OUR CARAVAN CROSSING THE TERELCHE RIVER

ACROSS MONGOLIAN PLAINS

A NATURALIST'S ACCOUNT OF
CHINA'S "GREAT NORTHWEST"

BY

ROY CHAPMAN ANDREWS

ASSOCIATE CURATOR OF MAMMALS IN THE AMERICAN MUSEUM OF NATURAL
HISTORY, AND LEADER OF THE MUSEUM'S SECOND ASIATIC EXPE-
DITION. AUTHOR OF "WHALE HUNTING WITH GUN AND
CAMERA," "CAMPS AND TRAILS IN CHINA," ETC.

PHOTOGRAPHS BY
YVETTE BORUP ANDREWS
Photographer of the
Second Asiatic Expedition

Fredonia Books
Amsterdam, The Netherlands

Across Mongolian Plains
A naturalist's account of China's
"Great Northwest"

by
Roy Chapman Andrews
Photographs by Yvette Borup Andrews

ISBN 1-58963-042-4

Reprinted from the 1921 edition

Fredonia Books
Amsterdam, The Netherlands
http://www.FredoniaBooks.com

THIS BOOK IS AFFECTIONATELY DEDICATED TO

Dr. J. A. ALLEN

WHO, THROUGH HIS PROFOUND KNOWLEDGE, UNSELFISH
DEVOTION TO SCIENCE, AND NEVER-FAILING SYMPATHY
WITH YOUNGER STUDENTS OF ZOÖLOGY HAS
BEEN AN EXAMPLE AND AN INSPIRATION DURING
THE YEARS I HAVE WORKED AT HIS SIDE.

PREFACE

During 1916–1917 the First Asiatic Expedition of the American Museum of Natural History carried on zoölogical explorations along the frontiers of Tibet and Burma in the little known province of Yün-nan, China. The narrative of that expedition has already been given to the public in the first book of this series "Camps and Trails in China." It was always the intention of the American Museum to continue the Asiatic investigations, and my presence in China on other work in 1918 gave the desired opportunity at the conclusion of the war.

Having made extensive collections along the southeastern edge of the great central Asian plateau, it was especially desirable to obtain a representation of the fauna from the northeastern part in preparation for the great expedition which, I am glad to say, is now in course of preparation, and which will conduct work in various other branches of science. Consequently, my wife and I spent one of the most delightful years of our lives in Mongolia and North China on the Second Asiatic Expedition of the American Museum of Natural History.

The present book is the narrative of our work and travels. As in "Camps and Trails" I have written it entirely from the sportsman's standpoint and have purposely avoided scientific details which would prove uninteresting or wearisome to the general public. Full reports of the expedition's results will appear in due course in the Museum's scientific publications and to them I would refer those readers who wish further details of the Mongolian fauna.

Asia is the most fascinating hunting ground in all the world, not because of the *quantity* of game to be found there but because of its *quality*, and scientific importance. Central Asia was the point of origin and distribution for many mammals which inhabit other parts of the earth to-day and the habits and relationships of some of its big game animals are almost unknown. Because of unceasing native persecution, lack of protection, the continued destruction of forests and the ever increasing facilities for transportation to the remote districts of the interior, many of China's most interesting and important forms of wild life are doomed to extermination in the very near future.

Fortunately world museums are awakening to the necessity of obtaining representative series of Asiatic mammals before it is too late, and to the broad vision of the President and Board of Trustees of the American Museum of Natural History my wife and I owe the exceptional opportunities which have been given us to carry on zoölogical explorations in Asia.

We are especially grateful to President Henry Fairfield Osborn, who is ready, always, to support enthusiastically any plans which tend to increase knowledge of China or to strengthen cordial relations between the United States and the Chinese Republic.

Director F. A. Lucas and Assistant Secretary George H. Sherwood have never failed in their attention to the needs of our expeditions when in the field and to them I extend our best thanks.

Mr. and Mrs. Charles L. Bernheimer, who have contributed to every expedition in which I have taken part, generously rendered financial aid for the Mongolian work.

My wife, who is ever my best assistant in the field, was responsible for all the photographic work of the expedition and I have drawn much upon her daily "Journals" in the preparation of this book.

I wish to acknowledge the kindness of the Editors of *Harper's Magazine*, *Natural History*, *Asia Magazine* and the *Trans-Pacific Magazine* in whose publications parts of this book have already appeared.

We are indebted to a host of friends who gave assistance to the expedition and to us personally in the field:

The Wai Chiao Pu (Ministry of Foreign Affairs) freely granted permits for the expedition to travel throughout China and extended other courtesies for which I wish to express appreciation on behalf of the President and Board of Trustees of the American Museum of Natural History.

In Peking, His Excellency Paul S. Reinsch, formerly American Minister to China, Dr. C. D. Tenney, Mr. Willys Peck, Mr. Ernest B. Price and other members of the Legation staff obtained import permits and attended to many details connected with the Chinese Government.

Mr. A. M. Guptil acted as our Peking representative while we were in the field and assumed much annoying detail in forwarding and receiving shipments of supplies and equipment. Other gentlemen in Peking who rendered us courtesies in various ways are Commanders I. V. Gillis and C. T. Hutchins, Dr. George D. Wilder, Dr. J. G. Anderson and Messrs. H. C. Faxon, E. G. Smith, C. R. Bennett, M. E. Weatherall and J. Kenrick.

In Kalgan, Mr. Charles L. Coltman arranged for the transportation of the expedition to Mongolia and not only gratuitously acted as our agent but was always ready to devote his own time and the use of his motor cars to further the work of the party.

In Urga, Mr. F. A. Larsen of Anderson, Meyer & Company, was of invaluable assistance in obtaining horses, carts and other equipment for the expedition as well as in giving us the benefit of his long and unique experience in Mongolia.

Mr. E. V. Olufsen of Anderson, Meyer & Company, put himself, his house, and his servants at our disposal whenever we were in Urga and aided us in innumerable ways.

Mr. and Mrs. Oscar Mamen often entertained us in their home. Mr. and Mrs. E. L. MacCallie, who accompanied us on one trip across Mongolia and later resided temporarily in Urga, brought equipment for us across Mongolia and entertained us while we were preparing to return to Peking.

Monsieur A. Orlow, Russian Diplomatic Agent in Urga, obtained permits from the Mongolian Government for our work in the Urga region and gave us much valuable advice.

In south China, Reverend H. Castle of Tunglu, and Reverend Lacy Moffet planned a delightful hunting trip for us in Che-kiang Province.

In Shanghai the Hon. E. S. Cunningham, American Consul-General, materially aided the expedition in the shipment of specimens. To Mr. G. M. Jackson, General Passenger Agent of the Canadian Pacific Ocean Services, thanks are due for arranging for rapid transportation to America of our valuable collections.

ROY CHAPMAN ANDREWS

AMERICAN MUSEUM OF
   NATURAL HISTORY,
NEW YORK CITY. U. S. A.

CONTENTS

CHAPTER VII

THE LONG TRAIL TO SAIN NOIN KHAN

CHAPTER VIII

THE LURE OF THE PLAINS

CHAPTER IX

HUNTING ON THE TURIN PLAINS

CHAPTER X

AN ADVENTURE IN THE LAMA CITY

CHAPTER XV

MONGOLIAN "ARGALI"

CHAPTER XVI

THE HORSE-DEER OF SHANSI

CHAPTER XVII

WAPITI, ROEBUCK AND GORAL

CHAPTER XVIII

WILD PIGS—ANIMAL AND HUMAN

ACROSS MONGOLIAN PLAINS

A NATURALIST'S ACCOUNT OF
CHINA'S "GREAT NORTHWEST"

INTRODUCTION

The romantic story of the Mongols and their achievements has been written so completely that it is unnecessary to repeat it here even though it is as fascinating as a tale from the *Arabian Nights*. The present status of the country, however, is but little known to the western world. In a few words I will endeavor to sketch the recent political developments, some of which occurred while we were in Mongolia.

In the twelfth and thirteenth centuries the great Genghiz Khan and his illustrious successor Kublai Khan "almost in a night" erected the greatest empire the world has ever seen. Not only did they conquer all of Asia, but they advanced in Europe as far as the Dnieper leaving behind a trail of blood and slaughter.

All Europe rose against them, but what could not be accomplished by force of arms was wrought in the Mongols themselves by an excess of luxury. In their victorious advance great stores of treasure fell into their hands and they gave themselves to a life of ease and indulgence.

By nature the Mongols were hard riding, hard living warriors, accustomed to privation and fatigue. The poison of luxury ate into the very fibers of their being and gradually they lost the characteristics which had made them great. The ruin of the race was completed by the introduction of Lamaism, a religion which carries only moral destruction where it enters, and eventually the Mongols passed under the rule of the once conquered Chinese and then under the Manchus.

Until the overthrow of the Manchu régime in China in 1911, and the establishment of the present republic, there were no particularly significant events in Mongolian history. But at that time the Russians, wishing to create a buffer state between themselves and China as well as to obtain special commercial privileges in Mongolia, aided the Mongols in rebellion, furnished them with arms and ammunition and with officers to train their men.

A somewhat tentative proclamation of independence for Outer Mongolia was issued in December, 1911, by the Hutukhtu and nobles of Urga, and the Chinese were driven out of the country with little difficulty. Beset with internal troubles, the Chinese paid but scant attention to Mongolian affairs until news was received in Peking in October, 1912, that M. Korostovetz, formerly Russian Minister to China, had arrived secretly in Urga and on November 3, 1912, had recognized the independence of Outer Mongolia on behalf of his Government.

It then became incumbent upon China to take official note of the situation, especially as foreign complications could not be faced in view of her domestic embarrassments.

Consequently on November 5, 1913, there was concluded a Russo-Chinese agreement wherein Russia recognized that Outer Mongolia was under the suzerainty of China, and China, on her part, admitted the autonomy of Outer Mongolia. The essential element in the situation was the fact that Russia stood behind the Mongols with money and arms and China's hand was forced at a time when she was powerless to resist.

Quite naturally, Mongolia's political status has been a sore point with China and it is hardly surprising that she should have awaited an opportunity to reclaim what she considered to be her own.

This opportunity arrived with the collapse of Russia and the spread of Bolshevism, for the Mongols were dependent upon Russia for material assistance in anything resembling military operations, although, as early as 1914, they had begun to realize that they were cultivating a dangerous friend. The Mongolian army, at the most, numbered only two or three thousand poorly equipped and undisciplined troops who would require money and organization before they could become an effective fighting force.

The Chinese were not slow to appreciate these conditions and General Hsu Shu-tseng, popularly known as "Little Hsu," by a clever bit of Oriental intrigue sent four thousand soldiers to Urga with the excuse of protecting the Mongols from a so-called threatened invasion of Buriats and brigands. A little later he himself arrived in a motor car and, when the stage was set, brought such pressure to bear upon the Hutukhtu and his Cabinet that they had no recourse except to cancel Mongolia's autonomy and ask to return to their former place under Chinese rule.

This they did on November 17, 1919, in a formal Memorial addressed to the President of the Chinese Republic, which is quoted below as it appeared in the Peking press, under date of November 24, 1919:

"We, the Ministers and Vice-Ministers [here follow their names and ranks] of all the departments of the autonomous Government of Outer Mongolia, and all the princes, dukes, hutukhtus and lamas and others resident at Urga, hereby jointly and severally submit the following petition for the esteemed perusal of His Excellency the President of the Republic of China:—

"Outer Mongolia has been a dependency of China since the reign of the Emperor Kang Hsi, remaining loyal for over two hundred years, the entire population, from princes and dukes down to the common people having enjoyed the blessings of peace. During the reign of the Emperor Tao Kwang changes in the established institutions, which were opposed to Mongolian sentiment, caused dissatisfaction which was aggravated by the corruption of the administration during the last days of the Manchu Dynasty. Taking advantage of this Mongolian dissatisfaction, foreigners instigated and assisted the independence movement. Upon the Kiakhta Convention being signed the autonomy of Outer Mongolia was held a *fait accompli*, China retaining an empty suzerainty while the officials and people of Outer Mongolia lost many of their old rights and privileges. Since the establishment of this autonomous government no progress whatsoever has been chronicled, the affairs of government being indeed plunged in a state of chaos, causing deep pessimism.

"Lately, chaotic conditions have also reigned supreme in Russia, reports of revolutionary elements threatening our frontiers having been frequently received. Moreover, since the Russians have no united government it is only natural that they are powerless to carry out the provisions of the treaties, and now that they have no control over their subjects the Buriat tribes have constantly conspired and coöperated with bandits, and repeatedly sent delegates to Urga urging our Government to join with them and form a Pan-Mongolian nation. That this propaganda work, so varied and so persistent, which aims at usurping Chinese suzerainty and undermining the autonomy of Outer Mongolia, does more harm than good to Outer Mongolia, our Government is well aware. The Buriats, with their bandit Allies, now considering us unwilling to espouse their cause, contemplate dispatching troops to violate our frontiers and to compel our submission. Furthermore, forces from the so-called White Army have forcibly occupied Tanu Ulianghai, an old possession of Outer Mongolia, and attacked both Chinese and Mongolian troops, this being followed by the entry of the Red Army, thus making the situation impossible.

"Now that both our internal and external affairs have reached such a climax, we, the members of the Government, in view of the present situation, have assembled all the princes, dukes, lamas and others and have held frequent meetings to discuss the question of our future welfare. Those present have been unanimously of the opinion that the old bonds of friendship having been restored our autonomy should be canceled, since Chinese and Mongolians are filled with a common purpose and ideal.

"The result of our decision has been duly reported to His Holiness the Bogdo Jetsun Dampa Hutukhtu Khan and has received his approval and support. Such being the position we now unanimously petition His Excellency the President that the old order of affairs be restored."

(Signed)

"Premier and Acting Minister of the Interior, Prince Lama Batma Torgoo.

"Vice-Minister, Prince of Tarkhan Puntzuk Cheilin.

"Vice-Minister, Great Lama of Beliktu, Prince Puntzuk Torgoo.

"Minister of Foreign Affairs, Duke Cheilin Torgoo.

"Vice-Minister, Dalai Prince Cheitantnun Lomour.

"Vice-Minister, Prince of Ochi, Kaotzuktanba.

"Minister of War, Prince of Eltoni Jamuyen Torgoo.

"Vice-Minister, Prince of Eltoni Selunto Chihloh.

"Vice-Minister, Prince of Elteni Punktzu Laptan.

"Vice-Minister, Prince of Itkemur Chitu Wachir.

"Minister of Finance, Prince Lama Loobitsan Paletan.

"Vice-Minister, Prince Torgee Cheilin.

"Vice-Minister, Prince of Suchuketu Tehmutgu Kejwan.

"Minister of Justice, Dalai of Chiechenkhan Wananin.

"Vice-Minister, Prince of Daichinchihlun Chackehbatehorhu.

"Vice-Minister, Prince of Cholikota Lama Dashtunyupu."

Naturally, the President of China graciously consented to allow the prodigal to return and "killed the fatted calf" by conferring high honors and titles upon the Hutukhtu. Moreover, he appointed the Living Buddha's good friend (?) "Little Hsu" to convey them to him.

Thus, Mongolia again has become a part of China. Who knows what the future has in store for her? But events are moving rapidly and by the time this book is published the curtain may have risen upon a new act of Mongolia's tragedy.

ACROSS MONGOLIAN PLAINS

CHAPTER I

ENTERING THE LAND OF MYSTERY

Careering madly in a motor car behind a herd of antelope fleeing like wind-blown ribbons across a desert which isn't a desert, past caravans of camels led by picturesque Mongol horsemen, the Twentieth Century suddenly and violently interjected into the Middle Ages, should be contrast and paradox enough for even the most *blasé* sportsman. I am a naturalist who has wandered into many of the far corners of the earth. I have seen strange men and things, but what I saw on the great Mongolian plateau fairly took my breath away and left me dazed, utterly unable to adjust my mental perspective.

When leaving Peking in late August, 1918, to cross the Gobi Desert in Mongolia, I knew that I was to go by motor car. But somehow the very names "Mongolia" and "Gobi Desert" brought such a vivid picture of the days of Kublai Khan and ancient Cathay that my clouded mind refused to admit the thought of automobiles. It was enough that I was going to the land of which I had so often dreamed.

1

Not even in the railway, when I was being borne toward Kalgan and saw lines of laden camels plodding silently along the paved road beside the train, or when we puffed slowly through the famous Nankou Pass and I saw that wonder of the world, the Great Wall, winding like a gray serpent over ridge after ridge of the mountains, was my dream-picture of mysterious Mongolia dispelled. I had seen all this before, and had accepted it as one accepts the motor cars beside the splendid walls of old Peking. It was too near, and the railroad had made it commonplace.

But Mongolia! That was different. One could not go there in a roaring train. I had beside me the same old rifle and sleeping bag that had been carried across the mountains of far Yün-nan, along the Tibetan frontier, and through the fever-stricken jungles of Burma. Somehow, these companions of forest and mountain trails, and my reception at Kalgan by two khaki-clad young men, each with a belt of cartridges and a six-shooter strapped about his waist, did much to keep me in a blissful state of unpreparedness for the destruction of my dream-castles.

That night as we sat in Mr. Charles Coltman's home, with his charming wife, a real woman of the great outdoors, presiding at the dinner table, the talk was all of shooting, horses, and the vast, lone spaces of the Gobi Desert—but not much of motor cars. Perhaps they vaguely realized that I was still asleep in an unreal world and knew that the awakening would come all too soon.

Yet I was dining that night with one of the men who had destroyed the mystery of Mongolia. In 1916, Coltman and his former partner, Oscar Mamen, had driven across the plains to Urga, the historic capital of Mongolia. But most unromantic and incongruous, most disheartening to a dreamer of Oriental dreams, was what I learned a few days later when the awakening had really come—that among the first cars ever to cross the desert was one purchased by the Hutukhtu, the Living Buddha, the God of all the Mongols.

When the Hutukhtu learned of the first motor car in Mongolia he forthwith demanded one for himself. So his automobile was brought safely through the rocky pass at Kalgan and across the seven hundred miles of plain to Urga by way of the same old caravan trail over which, centuries ago, Genghis Khan had sent his wild Mongol raiders to conquer China.

We arose long before daylight on the morning of August 29. In the courtyard lanterns flashed and disappeared like giant fireflies as the *mafus* (muleteers) packed the baggage and saddled the ponies. The cars had been left on the plateau at a mission station called Hei-ma-hou to avoid the rough going in the pass, and we were to ride there on horseback while the food and bed-rolls went by cart. There were five of us in the party—Mr. and Mrs. Coltman, Mr. and Mrs. Lucander, and myself. I was on a reconnoissance and Mr. Coltman's object was to visit his trading station in Urga, where the Lucanders were to remain for the winter.

The sun was an hour high when we clattered over the

slippery paving stones to the north gate of the city. Kalgan is built hard against the Great Wall of China— the first line of defense, the outermost rampart in the colossal structure which for so many centuries protected China from Tartar invasion. Beyond it there was nothing between us and the great plateau.

After our passports had been examined we rode through the gloomy chasm-like gate, turned sharply to the left, and found ourselves standing on the edge of a half-dry river bed. Below us stretched line after line of double-humped camels, some crowded in yellow-brown masses which seemed all heads and curving necks, and some kneeling quietly on the sand. From around a shoulder of rock came other camels, hundreds of them, treading slowly and sedately, nose to tail, toward the gate in the Great Wall. They had come from the far country whither we were bound. To me there is something fascinating about a camel. Perhaps it is because he seems to typify the great waste spaces which I love, that I never tire of watching him swing silently, and seemingly with resistless power, across the desert.

Our way to Hei-ma-hou led up the dry river bed, with the Great Wall on the left stretching its serpentine length across the hills, and on the right picturesque cliffs two hundred feet in height. At their bases nestle mud-roofed cottages and Chinese inns, but farther up the river the low hills are all of *loess*—brown, wind-blown dust, packed hard, which can be cut like cheese. Deserted though they seem from a distance, they really teem with human life. Whole villages are half dug, half built, into the hillsides, but are well-nigh invisible, for every wall and roof is of the same brown earth.

Ten miles or so from Kalgan we began on foot the long climb up the pass which gives entrance to the great plateau. I kept my eyes steadily on the pony's heels until we reached a broad, flat terrace halfway up the pass. Then I swung about that I might have, all at once, the view which lay below us. It justified my greatest hopes, for miles and miles of rolling hills stretched away to where the far horizon met the Shansi Mountains.

It was a desolate country which I saw, for every wave in this vast land-sea was cut and slashed by the knives of wind and frost and rain, and lay in a chaotic mass of gaping wounds—cañons, ravines, and gullies, painted in rainbow colors, crossing and cutting one another at fantastic angles as far as the eye could see.

When, a few moments later, we reached the very summit of the pass, I felt that no spot I had ever visited satisfied my preconceived conceptions quite so thoroughly. Behind and below us lay that stupendous relief map of ravines and gorges; in front was a limitless stretch of undulating plain. I knew then that I really stood upon the edge of the greatest plateau in all the world and that it could be only Mongolia.

We had tiffin at a tiny Chinese inn beside the road, and trotted on toward Hei-ma-hou between waving fields of wheat, buckwheat, millet, and oats—oats as thick and "meaty" as any horse could wish to eat.

After tiffin Coltman and Lucander rode rapidly ahead

while I trotted my pony along more slowly in the rear. It was nearly seven o'clock, and the trees about the mission station had been visible for half an hour. I was enjoying a gorgeous sunset which splashed the western sky with gold and red, and lazily watching the black silhouettes of a camel caravan swinging along the summit of a ridge a mile away. On the road beside me a train of laden mules and bullock-carts rested for a moment—the drivers half asleep. Over all the plain there lay the peace of a perfect autumn evening.

Suddenly, from behind a little rise, I heard the whir of a motor engine and the raucous voice of a Klaxon horn. Before I realized what it meant, I was in the midst of a mass of plunging, snorting animals, shouting carters, and kicking mules. In a moment the caravan scattered wildly across the plain and the road was clear save for the author of the turmoil—a black automobile.

I wish I could make those who spend their lives within a city know how strange and out of place that motor seemed, alone there upon the open plain on the borders of Mongolia. Imagine a camel or an elephant with all its Oriental trappings suddenly appearing on Fifth Avenue! You would think at once that it had escaped from a circus or a zoo and would be mainly curious as to what the traffic policeman would do when it did not obey his signals.

But all the incongruity and the fact that the automobile was a glaring anachronism did not prevent my abandoning my horse to the *mafu* and stretching out comfortably on the cushions of the rear seat. There I had nothing to do but collect the remains of my shattered dream-castles as we bounced over the ruts and stones. It was a rude awakening, and I felt half ashamed to admit to myself as the miles sped by that the springy seat was more comfortable than the saddle on my Mongol pony.

But that night when I strolled about the mission courtyard, under the spell of the starry, desert sky, I drifted back again in thought to the glorious days of Kublai Khan. My heart was hot with resentment that this thing had come. I realized then that, for better or for worse, the sanctity of the desert was gone forever. Camels will still plod their silent way across the age-old plains, but the mystery is lost. The secrets which were yielded up to but a chosen few are open now to all, and the world and his wife will speed their noisy course across the miles of rolling prairie, hearing nothing, feeling nothing, knowing nothing of that resistless desert charm which led men out into the Great Unknown.

At daylight we packed the cars. Bed-rolls and cans of gasoline were tied on the running boards and every corner was filled with food. Our rifles were ready for use, however, for Coltman had promised a kind of shooting such as I had never seen before. The stories he told of wild rides in the car after strings of antelope which traveled at fifty or sixty miles an hour had left me mildly skeptical. But then, you know, I had never seen a Mongolian antelope run.

For twenty or thirty miles after leaving Hei-ma-hou we bounced along over a road which would have been splendid except for the deep ruts cut by mule- and ox-carts. These carts are the despair of any one who hopes some time to see good roads in China. The spike-studded wheels cut into the hardest ground and leave a chaos of ridges and chasms which grows worse with every year.

We were seldom out of sight of mud-walled huts or tiny Chinese villages, and Chinese peddlers passed our cars, carrying baskets of fruit or trinkets for the women. Chinese farmers stopped to gaze at us as we bounded over the ruts—in fact it was all Chinese, although we were really in Mongolia. I was very eager to see Mongols, to register first impressions of a people of whom I had dreamed so much; but the blue-clad Chinaman was ubiquitous.

For seventy miles from Kalgan it was all the same—Chinese everywhere. The Great Wall was built to keep the Mongols out, and by the same token it should have kept the Chinese in. But the rolling, grassy sea of the vast plateau was too strong a temptation for the Chinese farmer. Encouraged by his own government, which knows the value of just such peaceful penetration, he pushes forward the line of cultivation a dozen miles or so every year. As a result the grassy hills have given place to fields of wheat, oats, millet, buckwheat, and potatoes.

The Mongol, above all things, is not a farmer; possibly because, many years ago, the Manchus forbade him to till the soil. Moreover, on the ground he is as awkward as a duck out of water and he is never comfortable.

The back of a pony is his real home, and he will do wonderfully well any work which keeps him in the saddle. As Mr. F. A. Larsen in Urga once said, "A Mongol would make a splendid cook if you could give him a horse to ride about on in the kitchen." So he leaves to the plodding Chinaman the cultivation of his boundless plains, while he herds his fat-tailed sheep and goats and cattle.

About two hours after leaving the mission station we passed the limit of cultivation and were riding toward the Tabool hills. There Mr. Larsen, the best known foreigner in all Mongolia, has a home, and as we swung past the trail which leads to his house we saw one of his great herds of horses grazing in the distance.

All the land in this region has long, rich grass in summer, and water is by no means scarce. There are frequent wells and streams along the road, and in the distance we often caught a glint of silver from the surface of a pond or lake. Flocks of goats and fat-tailed sheep drifted up the valley, and now and then a herd of cattle massed themselves in moving patches on the hillsides. But they are only a fraction of the numbers which this land could easily support.

Not far from Tabool is a Mongol village. I jumped out of the car to take a photograph but scrambled in again almost as quickly, for as soon as the motor had stopped a dozen dogs dashed from the houses snarling and barking like a pack of wolves. They are huge brutes, these Mongol dogs, and as fierce as they are big. Every family and every caravan owns one or more, and we learned very soon never to approach a native encampment on foot.

The village was as unlike a Chinese settlement as it well could be, for instead of closely packed mud houses there were circular, latticed frameworks covered with felt and cone-shaped in the upper half. The *yurt*, as it is called, is perfectly adapted to the Mongols and their life. In the winter a stove is placed in the center, and the house is dry and warm. In the summer the felt covering is sometimes replaced by canvas which can be lifted on any side to allow free passage of air. When it is time for the semiannual migration to new grazing grounds the *yurt* can be quickly dismantled, the framework collapsed, and the house packed on camels or carts.

The Mongols of the village were rather disappointing, for many of them show a strong element of Chinese blood. This seems to have developed an unfortunate combination of the worst characteristics of both races. Even where there is no real mixture, their contact with the Chinese has been demoralizing, and they will rob and steal at every opportunity. The headdresses of the southern women are by no means as elaborate as those in the north.

When the hills of Tabool had begun to sink on the horizon behind us, we entered upon a vast rolling plain, where there was but little water and not a sign of human life. It resembled nothing so much as the prairies of Nebraska or Dakota, and amid the short grass larkspur and purple thistles glowed in the sunlight like tongues of flame.

There was no lack of birds. In the ponds which we passed earlier in the day we saw hundreds of mallard ducks and teal. The car often frightened golden plover from their dust baths in the road, and crested lapwings flashed across the prairie like sudden storms of autumn leaves. Huge, golden eagles and enormous ravens made tempting targets on the telegraph poles, and in the morning before we left the cultivated area we saw demoiselle cranes in thousands.

In this land where wood is absent and everything that will make a fire is of value, I wondered how it happened that the telegraph poles remained untouched, for every one was smooth and round without a splinter gone. The method of protection is simple and entirely Oriental. When the line was first erected, the Mongolian government stated in an edict that any man who touched a pole with knife or ax would lose his head. Even on the plains the enforcement of such a law is not so difficult as it might seem, and after a few heads had been taken by way of example the safety of the line was assured.

Our camp the first night was on a hill slope about one hundred miles from Hei-ma-hou. As soon as the cars had stopped, one man was left to untie the sleeping bags while the rest of us scattered over the plain to hunt material for a fire. *Argul* (dried dung) forms the only desert fuel and, although it does not blaze like wood, it will "boil a pot" almost as quickly as charcoal. I was elected to be the cook—a position with distinct advantages, for in the freezing cold of early morning I could linger about the fire with a good excuse.

It was a perfect autumn night. Every star in the world of space seemed to have been crowded into our own particular expanse of sky, and each one glowed like a tiny lantern. When I had found a patch of sand and had dug a trench for my hip and shoulder, I crawled into the sleeping bag and lay for half an hour looking up at the bespangled canopy above my head. Again the magic of the desert night was in my blood, and I blessed the fate which had carried me away from the roar and rush of New York with its hurrying crowds. But I felt a pang of envy when, far away in the distance, there came the mellow notes of a camel-bell. *Dong, dong, dong* it sounded, clear and sweet as cathedral chimes. With surging blood I listened until I caught the measured tread of padded feet, and saw the black silhouettes of rounded bodies and curving necks. Oh, to be with them, to travel as Marco Polo traveled, and to learn to know the heart of the desert in the long night marches! Before I closed my eyes that night I vowed that when the war was done and I was free to travel where I willed, I would come again to the desert as the great Venetian came.

CHAPTER II

SPEED MARVELS OF THE GOBI DESERT

The next morning, ten miles from camp, we passed a party of Russians en route to Kalgan. They were sitting disconsolately beside two huge cars, patching tires and tightening bolts. Their way had been marked by a succession of motor troubles and they were almost discouraged. Woe to the men who venture into the desert with an untried car and without a skilled mechanic! There are no garages just around the corner—and there are no corners. Lucander's Chinese boy expressed it with laconic completeness when some one asked him how he liked the country.

"Well," said he, "there's plenty of *room* here."

A short distance farther on we found the caravan which had passed us early in the night. They were camped beside a well and the thirsty camels were gorging themselves with water. Except for these wells, the march across the desert would be impossible. They are four or five feet wide, walled with timbers, and partly roofed. In some the water is rather brackish but always cool, for it is seldom less than ten feet below the surface. It is useless to speculate as to who dug the wells or when, for this trail has been used for centuries. In some regions they are fifty or even sixty miles apart, but usually less than that.

The camel caravans travel mostly at night. For all his size and apparent strength, a camel is a delicate animal and needs careful handling. He cannot stand the heat of the midday sun and he will not graze at night. So the Gobi caravans start about three or four o'clock in the afternoon and march until one or two the next morning. Then the men pitch a light tent and the camels sleep or wander over the plain.

At noon on the second day we reached Panj-kiang, the first telegraph station on the line. Its single mud house was visible miles away and we were glad to see it, for our gasoline was getting low. Coltman had sent a plentiful supply by caravan to await us here, and every available inch of space was filled with cans, for we were only one-quarter of the way to Urga.

Not far beyond Panj-kiang, a lama monastery has been built beside the road. Its white-walled temple bordered with red and the compound enclosing the living quarters of the lamas show with startling distinctness on the open plain. We stopped for water at a well a few hundred yards away, and in five minutes the cars were surrounded by a picturesque group of lamas who streamed across the plain on foot and on horseback, their yellow and red robes flaming in the sun. They were amiable enough—in fact, too friendly—and their curiosity was hardly welcome, for we found one of them testing his knife on the tires and another about to punch a hole in one of the gasoline cans; he hoped it held something to drink that was better than water.

Thus far the trail had not been bad, as roads go in the Gobi, but I was assured that the next hundred miles would be a different story, for we were about to enter the most arid part of the desert between Kalgan and Urga. We were prepared for the only real work of the trip, however, by a taste of the exciting shooting which Coltman had promised me.

I had been told that we should see antelope in thousands, but all day I had vainly searched the plains for a sign of game. Ten miles from Panj-kiang we were rolling comfortably along on a stretch of good road when Mrs. Coltman, whose eyes are as keen as those of a hawk, excitedly pointed to a knoll on the right, not a hundred yards from the trail. At first I saw nothing but yellow grass; then the whole hillside seemed to be in motion. A moment later I began to distinguish heads and legs and realized that I was looking at an enormous herd of antelope, closely packed together, restlessly watching us.

Our rifles were out in an instant and Coltman opened the throttle. The antelope were five or six hundred yards away, and as the car leaped forward they ranged themselves in single file and strung out across the plain. We left the road at once and headed diagonally toward them. For some strange reason, when a horse or car runs parallel with a herd of antelope, the animals will swing in a complete semicircle and cross in front of the pursuer. This is also true of some African species.

Whether they think they are being cut off from some more desirable means of escape I cannot say, but the fact remains that with the open plain on every side they always try to "cross your bows."

I shall never forget the sight of those magnificent animals streaming across the desert! There were at least a thousand of them, and their yellow bodies seemed fairly to skim the earth. I was shouting in excitement, but Coltman said:

"They're not running yet. Wait till we begin to shoot."

I could hardly believe my eyes when I saw the speedometer trembling at thirty-five miles, for we were making a poor showing with the antelope. But then the fatal attraction began to assert itself and the long column bent gradually in our direction. Coltman widened the arc of the circle and held the throttle up as far as it would go. Our speed increased to forty miles and the car began to gain because the antelope were running almost across our course.

They were about two hundred yards away when Coltman shut off the gas and jammed both brakes, but before the car had stopped they had gained another hundred. I leaped over a pile of bedding and came into action with the .250 Savage high-power as soon as my feet were on the ground. Coltman's .30 Mauser was already spitting fire from the front seat across the windshield, and at his second shot an antelope dropped like lead. My first two bullets struck the dirt far behind the rearmost animal, but the third caught a full-grown female in the side and she plunged forward into the grass.

I realized then what Coltman meant when he said that the antelope had not begun to run. At the first shot every animal in the herd seemed to flatten itself and settle to its work. They did not run—they simply *flew* across the ground, their legs showing only as a blur. The one I killed was four hundred yards away, and I held four feet ahead when I pulled the trigger. They could not have been traveling less than fifty-five or sixty miles an hour, for they were running in a semicircle about the car while we were moving at forty miles in a straight line.

Those are the facts in the case. I can see my readers raise their brows incredulously, for that is exactly what I would have done before this demonstration. Well, there is one way to prove it and that is to come and try it for yourselves. Moreover, I can see some sportsmen smile for another reason. I mentioned that the antelope I killed was four hundred yards away. I know how far it was, for I paced it off. I may say, in passing, that I had never before killed a running animal at that range. Ninety per cent of my shooting had been well within one hundred and fifty yards, but in Mongolia conditions are most extraordinary.

In the brilliant atmosphere an antelope at four hundred yards appears as large as it would at one hundred in most other parts of the world; and on the flat plains, where there is not a bush or a shrub to obscure the view, a tiny stone stands out like a golf ball on the putting green. Because of these conditions there is strong temptation to shoot at impossible ranges and to keep on shooting when the game is beyond anything except a lucky chance. Therefore, if any of you go to Mongolia to hunt antelope take plenty of ammunition, and when you return you will never tell how many cartridges you used. Our antelope were tied on the running board of the car and we went back to the road where Lucander was waiting. Half the herd had crossed in front of him, but he had failed to bring down an animal.

When the excitement was over I began to understand the significance of what we had seen. It was slowly borne in upon me that our car had been going, by the speedometer, at forty miles an hour and that the *antelope were actually beating us*. It was an amazing discovery, for I had never dreamed that any living animal could run so fast. It was a discovery, too, which would have important results, for Professor Henry Fairfield Osborn, president of the American Museum of Natural History, even then was carrying on investigations as to the relation of speed to limb structure in various groups of animals. I determined, with Mr. Coltman's help, to get some real facts in the case—data upon which we could rely.

There was an opportunity only to begin the study on the first trip, but we carried it further the following year. Time after time, as we tore madly after antelope, singly or in herds, I kept my eyes upon the speedometer, and I feel confident that our observations can be relied upon. We demonstrated beyond a doubt that the Mongolian antelope can reach a speed of from fifty-five to sixty miles an hour. This is probably the maximum *which is attained only in the initial sprint* and after a very short distance the animals must slow down to about forty miles; a short distance more and they drop to twenty-five or thirty miles, and at this pace they seem able to continue almost indefinitely. They never ran faster than was necessary to keep well away from us. As we opened the throttle of the car they, too, increased their speed. It was only when we began to shoot and they became thoroughly frightened that they showed what they could do.

I remember especially one fine buck which gave us an exhibition of really high-class running. He started almost opposite to us when we were on a stretch of splendid road and jogged comfortably along at thirty-five miles an hour. Our car was running at the same speed, but he decided to cross in front and pressed his accelerator a little. Coltman also touched ours, and the motor jumped to forty miles. The antelope seemed very much surprised and gave his accelerator another push. Coltman did likewise, and the speedometer registered forty-five miles. That was about enough for us, and we held our speed. The animal drew ahead on a long curve swinging across in front of the car. He had beaten us by a hundred yards!

But we had a surprise in store for him, for Coltman suddenly shut off the gas and threw on both brakes. Before the motor had fully stopped we opened fire. The first two bullets struck just behind the antelope and a third kicked the dust between his legs. The shock turned him half over, but he righted himself and ran to his very limit. The bullets spattering all about kept him at it for six hundred yards. He put up a desert hare on the way, but that hare didn't have a chance with the antelope. It reminded me of the story of the negro who had seen a ghost. He ran until he dropped beside the road, but the ghost was right beside him. "Well," said the ghost, "that was *some* race we had." "Yes," answered the negro, "but it ain't nothin' to what we're goin' to have soon's ever I git my breath. And then," said the negro, "we ran agin. And I come to a rabbit leggin' it up the road, and I said, 'Git out of the way, rabbit, and let some one run what *can* run!' " The last we saw of the antelope was a cloud of yellow dust disappearing over a low rise.

The excitement of the chase had been an excellent preparation for the hard work which awaited us not far ahead. The going had been getting heavier with every mile, and at last we reached a long stretch of sandy road which the motors could not pull through. With every one except the driver out of the car, and the engine racing, we pushed and lifted, gaining a few feet each time, until the shifting sand was passed. It meant two hours of violent strain, and we were well-nigh exhausted; a few miles farther, however, it had all to be done again. Where the ground was hard, there was such a chaos of ruts and holes that our arms were almost wrenched from their sockets by the twisting wheels.

This area more nearly approaches a desert than any other part of the road to Urga. The soil is mainly sandy, but the Gobi sagebrush and short bunch grass, although sparse and dry, still give a covering of vegetation, so that in the distance the plain appears like a rolling meadowland.

When we saw our first northern Mongol I was delighted. Every one is a study for an artist. He dresses in a long, loose robe of plum color, one corner of which is usually tucked into a gorgeous sash. On his head is perched an extraordinary hat which looks like a saucer, with upturned edges of black velvet and a narrow cone-shaped crown of brilliant yellow. Two streamers of red ribbon are usually fastened to the rim at the back, or a plume of peacock feathers if he be of higher rank.

On his feet he wears a pair of enormous leather boots with pointed toes. These are always many sizes too large, for as the weather grows colder he pads them out with heavy socks of wool or fur. It is nearly impossible for him to walk in this ungainly footgear, and he waddles along exactly like a duck. He is manifestly uncomfortable and ill at ease, but put him on a horse and you have a different picture. The high-peaked saddle and the horse itself become a part of his anatomy and he will stay there happily fifteen hours of the day.

The Mongols ride with short stirrups and, standing nearly upright, lean far over the horse's neck like our western cowboys. As they tear along at full gallop in their brilliant robes they seem to embody the very spirit of the plains. They are such genial, accommodating fellows, always ready with a pleasant smile, and willing to take a sporting chance on anything under the sun, that they won my heart at once.

Above all things they love a race, and often one of them would range up beside the car and, with a radiant smile, make signs that he wished to test our speed. Then off he would go like mad, flogging his horse and yelling with delight. We would let him gain at first, and the expression of joy and triumph on his face was worth going far to see. Sometimes, if the road was heavy, it would need every ounce of gas the car could take to forge ahead, for the ponies are splendid animals. The Mongols ride only the best and ride them hard, since horses are cheap in Mongolia, and when one is a little worn another is always ready.

Not only does the Mongol inspire you with admiration for his full-blooded, virile manhood, but also you like him because he likes you. He doesn't try to disguise the fact. There is a frank openness about his attitude which is wonderfully appealing, and I believe that the average white man can get on terms of easy familiarity, and even intimacy, with Mongols more rapidly than with any other Orientals.

Ude is the second telegraph station on the road to Urga. It has the honor of appearing on most maps of Mongolia and yet it is even less impressive than Panjkiang. There are only two mud houses and half a dozen *yurts* which seem to have been dropped carelessly behind a ragged hill.

After leaving Ude, we slipped rapidly up and down a succession of low hills and entered upon a plain so

vast and flat that we appeared to be looking across an
ocean. Not the smallest hill or rise of ground broke the
line where earth and sky met in a faint blue haze. Our
cars seemed like tiny boats in a limitless, grassy sea. It
was sixty miles across, and for three hours the steady
hum of the motor hardly ceased, for the road was smooth
and hard. Halfway over we saw another great herd of
antelope and several groups of ten or twelve. These
were a different species from those we had killed, and I
got a fine young buck. Twice wolves trotted across the
plain, and at one, which was very inquisitive, I did some
shooting which I vainly try to forget.

But most interesting to me among the wild life along
our way was the bustard. It is a huge bird, weighing
from fifteen to forty pounds, with flesh of such delicate
flavor that it rivals our best turkey. I had always
wanted to kill a bustard and my first one was neatly
eviscerated at two hundred yards by a Savage bullet.
I was more pleased than if I had shot an antelope, perhaps because it did much to revive my spirits after the
episode of the wolf.

Sand grouse, beautiful little gray birds, with wings
like pigeons and remarkable, padded feet, whistled over
us as we rolled along the road, and my heart was sick
with the thought of the excellent shooting we were missing. But there was no time to stop, except for such
game as actually crossed our path, else we should never
have arrived at Urga, the City of the Living God.

Speaking of gods, I must not forget to mention the
great lamasery at Turin, about one hundred and seventy

miles from Urga. For hours before we reached it we saw the ragged hills standing sharp and clear against the sky line. The peaks themselves are not more than two hundred feet in height, but they rise from a rocky plateau some distance above the level of the plain. It is a wild spot where some mighty internal force has burst the surface of the earth and pushed up a ragged core of rocks which have been carved by the knives of weather into weird, fantastic shapes. This elemental battle ground is a fit setting for the most remarkable group of human habitations that I have ever seen.

Three temples lie in a bowl-shaped hollow, surrounded by hundreds upon hundreds of tiny pill-box dwellings painted red and white. There must be a thousand of them and probably twice as many lamas. On the outskirts of the "city" to the south enormous piles of *argul* have been collected by the priests and bestowed as votive offerings by devout travelers. Vast as the supply seemed, it would take all this, and more, to warm the houses of the lamas during the bitter winter months when the ground is covered with snow. On the north the hills throw protecting arms about the homes of these half-wild men, who have chosen to spend their lives in this lonely desert stronghold. The houses are built of sawn boards, the first indication we had seen that we were nearing a forest country.

The remaining one hundred and seventy miles to Urga are a delight, even to the motorist who loves the paved roads of cities. They are like a boulevard amid glorious, rolling hills luxuriant with long, sweet grass.

In the distance herds of horses and cattle grouped themselves into moving patches, and fat-tailed sheep dotted the plain like drifts of snow. I have seldom seen a better grazing country. It needed but little imagination to picture what it will be a few years hence when the inevitable railroad claims the desert as its own, for this rich land cannot long remain untenanted. It was here that we saw the first marmots, an unfailing indication that we were in a northern country.

The thick blackness of a rainy night had enveloped us long before we swung into the Urga Valley and groped our way along the Tola River bank toward the glimmering lights of the sacred city. It seemed that we would never reach them, for twice we took the wrong turn and found ourselves in a maze of sandy bottoms and half-grown trees. But at ten o'clock we plowed through the mud of a narrow street and into the court-yard of the Mongolian Trading Company's home.

Oscar Mamen, Coltman's former partner, and Mrs. Mamen had spent several years there, and for six weeks they had had as guests Messrs. A. M. Guptil and E. B. Price, of Peking. Mr. Guptil was representing the American Military Attaché, and Mr. Price, Assistant Chinese Secretary of the American Legation, had come to Urga to establish communication with our consul at Irkutsk who had not been heard from for more than a month.

Urga recently had been pregnant with war possibilities. In the Lake Baikal region of Siberia there were several thousand Magyars and many Bolsheviki. It was known that Czechs expected to attack them, and that they would certainly be driven across the borders into Mongolia if defeated. In that event what would be the attitude of the Mongolian government? Would it intern the belligerents, or allow them to use the Urga district as a base of operations?

As a matter of fact, the question had been settled just before my arrival. The Czechs had made the expected attack with about five hundred men; all the Magyars, to the number of several thousand, had surrendered, and the Bolsheviki had disappeared like mists before the sun. The front of operations had moved in a single night almost two thousand miles away to the Omsk district, and it was certain that Mongolia would be left in peace. Mr. Price's work also was done, for the telegraph from Urga to Irkutsk was again in operation and thus communication was established with Peking.

The morning after my arrival Mr. Guptil and I rode out to see the town. Never have I visited such a city of contrasts, or one to which I was so eager to return. As we did come back, I shall tell, in a future chapter, of what we found there.

CHAPTER III

A CHAPTER OF ACCIDENTS

This is a "hard luck" chapter. Stories of ill-fortune are not always interesting, but I am writing this one to show what *can* happen to an automobile in the Gobi. We had gone to Urga without even a puncture and I began to feel that motoring in Mongolia was as simple as riding on Fifth Avenue—more so, in fact, for we did not have to watch traffic policemen or worry about "right of way." There is no crowding on the Gobi Desert. When we passed a camel caravan or a train of oxcarts we were sure to have plenty of room, for the landscape was usually spotted in every direction with fleeing animals.

Our motors had "purred" so steadily that accidents and repair shops seemed very far away and not of much importance. On the return trip, however, the reverse of the picture was presented and I learned that to be alone in the desert when something is wrong with the digestion of your automobile can have its serious aspects. Unless you are an expert mechanic and have an assortment of "spare parts," you may have to walk thirty or forty miles to the nearest water and spend many days of waiting until help arrives.

Fortunately for us, there are few things which either

Coltman or Guptil do not know about the "insides" of
a motor and, moreover, after a diagnosis, they both have
the ingenuity to remedy almost any trouble with a ham-
mer and a screw driver.

Four days after our arrival in Urga we left on the
return trip. As occupants of his car Charles Coltman
had Mr. Price, Mrs. Coltman, and Mrs. Mamen. With
the spiritual and physical assistance of Mr. Guptil I
drove the second automobile, carrying in the rear seat
a wounded Russian Cossack and a French-Czech, both
couriers. The third car was a Ford *chassis* to which a
wooden body had been affixed. It was designed to give
increased carrying space, but it looked like a half-grown
hayrack and was appropriately called the "agony box."
This was driven by a chauffeur named Wang and carried Mamen's Chinese house boy and an *amah* besides a
miscellaneous assortment of baggage.

It was a cold, gray morning when we started, with a
cutting wind sweeping down from the north, giving a
hint of the bitter winter which in another month would
hold all Mongolia in an icy grasp. We made our way
eastward up the valley to the Russian bridge across the
Tola River and pointed the cars southward on the caravan trail to Kalgan.

Just as we reached the summit of the second long hill,
across which the wind was sweeping in a glacial blast,
there came a rasping crash somewhere in the motor of
my car, followed by a steady *knock, knock, knock.*
"That's a connecting rod as sure as fate," said "Gup."
"We'll have to stop." When he had crawled under the

car and found that his diagnosis was correct, he said a few other things which ought to have relieved his mind considerably.

There was nothing to be done except to replace the broken part with a spare rod. For three freezing hours Gup and Coltman lay upon their backs under the car, while the rest of us gave what help we could. To add to the difficulties a shower of hail swept down upon us with all the fury of a Mongolian storm. It was three o'clock in the afternoon before we were ready to go on, and our camp that night was only sixty miles from Urga.

The next day as we passed Turin the Czech pointed out the spot where he had lain for three days and nights with a broken collar bone and a dislocated shoulder. He had come from Irkutsk carrying important dispatches and had taken passage in an automobile belonging to a Chinese company which with difficulty was maintaining a passenger service between Urga and Kalgan. As usual, the native chauffeur was dashing along at thirty-five miles an hour when he should not have driven faster than twenty at the most. One of the front wheels slid into a deep rut, the car turned completely over and the resulting casualties numbered one man dead and our Czech seriously injured. It was three days before another car carried him back to Urga, where the broken bones were badly set by a drunken Russian doctor. The Cossack, too, had been shot twice in the heavy fighting on the Russian front, and, although his wounds were barely healed, he had just ridden three hundred miles on horseback with dispatches for Peking.

Both my passengers were delighted to have escaped the Chinese motors, for in them accidents had been the rule rather than the exception. During one year nineteen cars had been smashed and lay in masses of twisted metal beside the road. The difficulty had been largely due to the native chauffeurs. Although these men can drive a car, they have no mechanical training and danger signals from the motor are entirely disregarded. Moreover, all Chinese dearly love "show" and the chauffeurs delight in driving at tremendous speed over roads where they should exercise the greatest care. The deep cart ruts are a continual menace, for between them the road is often smooth and fine. But a stone or a tuft of grass may send one of the front wheels into a rut and capsize the car. Even with the greatest care accidents will happen, and motoring in Mongolia is by no means devoid of danger and excitement.

About three o'clock in the afternoon of the second day we saw frantic signals from the agony box which had been lumbering along behind us. It appeared that the right rear wheel was broken and the car could go no farther. There was nothing for it but to camp right where we were while Charles repaired the wheel. Gup and I ran twenty miles down the road to look for a well, but without success. The remaining water was divided equally among us but next morning we discovered that the Chinese had secreted two extra bottles for themselves, while we had been saving ours to the last drop. It taught me a lesson by which I profited the following summer.

On the third day the agony box limped along until noon, but when we reached a well in the midst of the great plain south of Turin it had to be abandoned, while we went on to Ude, the telegraph station in the middle of the desert, and wired Mamen to bring a spare wheel from Urga.

The fourth day there was more trouble with the connecting rod on my car and we sat for two hours at a well while the motor was eviscerated and reassembled. It had ceased to be a joke, especially to Coltman and Guptil, for all the work fell upon them. By this time they were almost unrecognizable because of dirt and grease and their hands were cut and blistered. But they stood it manfully, and at each new accident Gup rose to greater and greater heights of oratory.

We were halfway between Ude and Panj-kiang when we saw two automobiles approaching from the south. Their occupants were foreigners we were sure, and as they stopped beside us a tall young man came up to my car. "I am Langdon Warner," he said. We shook hands and looked at each other curiously. Warner is an archæologist and Director of the Pennsylvania Museum. For ten years we had played a game of hide and seek through half the countries of the Orient and it seemed that we were destined never to meet each other. In 1910 I drifted into the quaint little town of Naha in the Loo-Choo Islands, that forgotten kingdom of the East. At that time it was far off the beaten track and very few foreigners had sought it out since 1854, when Commodore Perry negotiated a treaty with its king in the picturesque old Shuri Palace. Only a few months before I arrived, Langdon Warner had visited it on a collecting trip and the natives had not yet ceased to talk about the strange foreigner who gave them new baskets for old ones.

A little later Warner preceded me to Japan, and in 1912 I followed him to Korea. Our paths diverged when I went to Alaska in 1913, but I crossed his trail again in China, and in 1916, just before my wife and I left for Yün-nan, I missed him in Boston where I had gone to lecture at Harvard University. It was strange that after ten years we should meet for the first time in the middle of the Gobi Desert!

Warner was proceeding to Urga with two Czech officers who were on their way to Irkutsk. We gave them the latest news of the war situation and much to their disgust they realized that had they waited only two weeks longer they could have gone by train, for the attack by the Czechs on the Magyars and the Bolsheviki, in the trans-Baikal region, had cleared the Siberian railway westward as far as Omsk. After half an hour's talk we drove off in opposite directions. Warner eventually reached Irkutsk, but not without some interesting experiences with Bolsheviki along the way, and I did not see him again until last March (1920), when he came to my office in the American Museum just after we had returned to New York.

When we reached Panj-kiang we felt that our motor troubles were at an end, but ten miles beyond the station my car refused to pull through a sand pit and we found that there was trouble with the differential. It was necessary to dismantle the rear end of the car, and Coltman and Gup were well-nigh discouraged. The delay was a serious matter for I had urgent business in Japan, and it was imperative that I reach Peking as soon as possible. Charles finally decided to send me, together with Price, the Czech, and the Cossack, in his car, while he and Gup remained with the two ladies to repair mine.

Price and I drove back to Panj-kiang to obtain extra food and water for the working party and to telegraph Kalgan for assistance. We took only a little tea, macaroni, and two tins of sausage, for we expected to reach the mission station at Hei-ma-hou early the next morning.

We were hardly five miles from the broken car when we discovered that there was no more oil for our motor. It was impossible to go much farther and we decided that the only alternative was to wait until the relief party, for which we had wired, arrived from Kalgan. Just then the car swung over the summit of a rise, and we saw the white tent and grazing camels of an enormous caravan. Of course, Mongols would have mutton fat and why not use that for oil! The caravan leader assured us that he had fat in plenty and in ten minutes a great pot of it was warming over the fire.

We poured it into the motor and proceeded merrily on our way. But there was one serious obstacle to our enjoyment of that ride. Events had been moving so rapidly that we had eaten nothing since breakfast, and when a delicious odor of roast lamb began to arise from the motor, we realized that we were all very hungry. Dry macaroni would hardly do and the sausage must be saved for dinner. All the afternoon that tantalizing odor hovered in the air and I began to imagine that I could even smell mint sauce.

At six o'clock we saw the first *yurt* and purchased a supply of *argul* so that we could save time in making camp. The lamps of the car were *hors de combat* and a watery moon did not give us sufficient light by which to drive in safety, so we stopped on a hilltop shortly after dark. In the morning when the motor was cold we could save time and strength in cranking by pushing it down the slope.

Much to our disgust we found that the *argul* we had purchased from the Mongol was so mixed with dirt that it would not burn. After half an hour of fruitless work I gave up, and we divided the tin of cold sausage. It was a pretty meager dinner for four hungry men and I retired into my sleeping bag to dream of roast lamb and mint sauce. When the Cossack officer found that he was not to have his tea he was like a child with a stick of candy just out of reach. He tried to sleep but it was no use, and in half an hour I opened my eyes to see him flat on his face blowing lustily at a piece of *argul* which he had persuaded to emit a faint glow. For two mortal hours the Russian nursed that fire until his pot of water reached the boiling point. Then he insisted that we all wake up to share his triumph.

We reached the mission station at noon next day, and

Father Weinz, the Belgian priest in charge, gave us the first meal we had had in thirty-six hours. The Czech courier decided to remain at Hei-ma-hou and go in next day by cart, but we started immediately on the forty-mile horseback ride to Kalgan. A steady rain began about two o'clock in the afternoon, and in half an hour we were soaked to the skin; then the ugly, little gray stallion upon which I had been mounted planted both hind feet squarely on my left leg as we toiled up a long hill-trail to the pass, and I thought that my walking days had ended for all time. At the foot of the pass we halted at a dirty inn where they told us it would be useless to go on to Kalgan, for the gates of the city would certainly be closed and it would be impossible to enter until morning. There was no alternative except to spend the night at the inn, but as they had only a grass fire which burned out as soon as the cooking was finished, and as all our clothes were soaked, we spent sleepless hours shivering with cold.

The Cossack spoke only Mongol and Russian, and, as neither of us knew a single word of either language, it was difficult to communicate our plans to him. Finally, we found a Chinaman who spoke Mongol and who consented to act as interpreter. The natives at the inn could not understand why we were not able to talk to the Cossack. Didn't all white men speak the same language? Mr. Price endeavored to explain that Russian and English differ as much as do Chinese and Mongol, but they only smiled and shook their heads.

In the morning I was so stiff from the kick which the

gray stallion had given me that I could get to his back only with the greatest difficulty, but we reached Kalgan at eight o'clock. Unfortunately, the Cossack had left his passport in the cart which was to follow with his baggage, and the police at the gate would not let us pass. Mr. Price was well known to them and offered to assume responsibility for the Cossack in the name of the American Legation, but the policemen, who were much disgruntled at being roused so early in the morning, refused to let us enter.

Their attitude was so obviously absurd that we agreed to take matters into our own hands. We strolled outside the house and suddenly jumped on our horses. The sentries made a vain attempt to catch our bridle reins and we rode down the street at a sharp trot. There was another police station in the center of the city which it was impossible to avoid and as we approached it we saw a line of soldiers drawn up across the road. Our friends at the gate had telephoned ahead to have us stopped. Without hesitating we kept on, riding straight at the gray-clad policemen. With wildly waving arms they shouted at us to halt, but we paid not the slightest attention, and they had to jump aside to avoid being run down. The spectacle which these Chinese soldiers presented, as they tried to arrest us, was so ridiculous that we roared with laughter. Imagine what would happen on Fifth Avenue if you disregarded a traffic policeman's signal to stop!

Although the officials knew that we could be found at Mr. Coltman's house, we heard nothing further from the incident. It was so obviously a matter of personal ill nature on the part of the captain in charge of the gate police that they realized it was not a subject for further discussion.

After the luxury of a bath and shave we proceeded to Peking. Charles and Gup had rather a beastly time getting in. The car could not be repaired sufficiently to carry on under its own power, and, through a misunderstanding, the relief party only went as far as the pass and waited there for their arrival. They eventually found it necessary to hire three horses to tow them to the mission station where the "hard luck" story ended.

CHAPTER IV

NEW TRAVELS ON AN OLD TRAIL

The winter of 1918-19 we spent in and out of one of the most interesting cities in the world. Peking, with its background of history made vividly real by its splendid walls, its age-old temples and its mysterious Forbidden City, has a personality of its own.

When we had been away for a month or two there was always a delightful feeling of anticipation in returning to the city itself and to our friends in its cosmopolitan community.

Moreover, at our house in Wu Liang Tajen Hutung, a baby boy and his devoted nurse were waiting to receive us. Even at two years the extraordinary facility with which he discovered frogs and bugs, which, quite unknown to us, dwelt in the flower-filled courtyard, showed the hereditary instincts of a born explorer.

That winter gave us an opportunity to see much of ancient China, for we visited Shantung, traveled straight across the Provinces of Honan and Hupeh, and wandered about the mountains of Che-kiang on a serow hunt.

In February the equipment for our summer's work in Mongolia was on its way across the desert by caravan. We had sent flour, bacon, coffee, tea, sugar, but-

ter and dried fruit, for these could be purchased in
Urga only at prohibitive prices. Even then, with
camel charges at fourteen cents a *cattie* (1⅓ lbs.), a
fifty-pound sack of flour cost us more than six dollars
by the time it reached Urga.

Charles Coltman at Kalgan very kindly relieved me
of all the transportation details. We had seen him
several times in Peking during the winter, and had
planned the trip across the plains to Urga as *une belle
excursion.*

Mrs. Coltman was going, of course, as were Mr. and
Mrs. "Ted" MacCallie of Tientsin. "Mac" was a famous Cornell football star whom I knew by reputation
in my own college days. He was to take a complete
Delco electric lighting plant to Urga, with the hope
of installing it in the palace of the "Living God."

A soldier named Owen from the Legation guard
in Peking was to drive the Delco car, and I had two
Chinese taxidermists, Chen and Kang, besides Lü, our
cook and camp boy.

Chen had been loaned to me by Dr. J. G. Andersson,
Mining Adviser to the Chinese Republic, and proved
to be one of the best native collectors whom I have ever
employed. The Coltmans and MacCallies were to stay
only a few days in Urga, but they helped to make the
trip across Mongolia one of the most delightful parts
of our glorious summer.

We left Kalgan on May 17. Mac, Owen, and I rode
the forty miles to Hei-ma-hou on horseback while
Charles drove a motor occupied by the three women.

There is a circuitous route by which cars can cross the pass under their own power, but Coltman preferred the direct road and sent four mules to tow the automobile up the mountains to the edge of the plateau.

It was the same trail I had followed the previous September. Then, as I stood on the summit of the pass gazing back across the far, dim hills, my heart was sad for I was about to enter a new land alone. My "best assistant" was on the ocean coming as fast as steam could carry her to join me in Peking. I wondered if Fate's decree would bring us here together that we might both have, as a precious heritage for future years, the memories of this strange land of romance and of mystery. Now the dream had been fulfilled and never have I entered a new country with greater hopes of what it would bring to me. Never, too, have such hopes been more gloriously realized.

We packed the cars that night and at half past five the next morning were on the road. The sky was gray and cloud-hung, but by ten o'clock the sun burned out and we gradually emerged from the fur robes in which we had been buried.

Instead of the fields of ripening grain which in the previous autumn had spread the hills with a flowing golden carpet, we saw blue-clad Chinese farmers turning long brown furrows with homemade plows. The trees about the mission station had just begun to show a tinge of green—the first sign of awakening at the touch of spring from the long winter sleep. Already caravans were astir, and we passed lines of laden camels

now almost at the end of the long journey from Outer
Mongolia, whither we were bound. But, instead of
splendid beasts with upstanding humps and full neck
beards, the camels now were pathetic mountains of almost naked skin on which the winter hair hung in ragged
patches. The humps were loose and flat and flapped
disconsolately as the great bodies lurched along the
trail.

When we passed one caravan a *débonnaire* old Mongol wearing a derby hat swung out of line and
signaled us to stop. After an appraising glance at
the car he smiled broadly and indicated that he would
like to race. In a moment he was off yelling at the top
of his lungs and belaboring the bony sides of his camel
with feet and hands. The animal's ungainly legs
swung like a windmill in every direction it seemed, except forward, and yet the Mongol managed to keep his
rolling old "ship of the desert" abreast of us for several minutes. Finally we let him win the race, and
his look of delight was worth going far to see as he
waved us good-by and with a hearty *"sai-bei-nah"* loped
slowly back to the caravan.

The road was much better than it had been the previous fall. During the winter the constant tramp of
padded feet had worn down and filled the ruts which
had been cut by the summer traffic of spike-wheeled
carts. But the camels had almost finished their winter's
work. In a few weeks they would leave the trail to ox
and pony caravans and spend the hot months in idle-

ness, storing quantities of fat in their great hump reservoirs.

There was even more bird life than I had seen the previous September. The geese had all flown northward where we would find them scattered over their summer breeding grounds, but thousands of demoiselle cranes (*Anthropoides virgo*) had taken their places in the fields. They were in the midst of the spring courting and seemed to have lost all fear. One pair remained beside the road until we were less than twenty feet away, stepping daintily aside only when we threatened to run them down. Another splendid male performed a love dance for the benefit of his prospective bride quite undisturbed by the presence of our cars. With half-spread wings he whirled and leaped about the lady while every feather on her slim, blue body expressed infinite boredom and indifference to his passionate appeal.

Ruddy sheldrakes, mallards, shoveler ducks, and teal were in even the smallest ponds and avocets with sky-blue legs and slender recurved bills ran along the shores of a lake at which we stopped for tiffin. When we had passed the last Chinese village and were well in the Mongolian grasslands we had great fun shooting gophers (*Citellus mongolicus umbratus*) from the cars. It was by no means easy to kill them before they slipped into their dens, and I often had to burrow like a terrier to pull them out even when they were almost dead.

We got eighteen, and camped at half past four in order that the taxidermists might have time to prepare the skins. There was a hint of rain in the air and we pitched the tent for emergencies, although none of us wished to sleep inside. Mac suggested that we utilize the electric light plant even if we were on the Mongolian plains. In half an hour he had installed wires in the tent and placed an arc lamp on the summit of a pole. It was an extraordinary experience to see the canvas walls about us, to hear the mournful wail of a lone wolf outside, and yet be able to turn the switch of an electric light as though we were in the city. No arc lamp on Fifth Avenue blazed more brightly than did this one on the edge of the Gobi Desert where none of its kind had ever shone before. With the motor cars which had stolen the sanctity of the plains it was only another evidence of the passing of Mongolian mystery.

Usually when we camped we could see, almost immediately, the silhouettes of approaching Mongols black against the evening sky. Where they came from we could never guess. For miles there might not have been the trace of a human being, but suddenly they would appear as though from out the earth itself. Perhaps they had been riding along some distant ridge far beyond the range of white men's eyes, or the roar of a motor had carried to their ears across the miles of plain; or perhaps it was that unknown sense, which seems to have been developed in these children of the desert, which directs them unerringly to water, to a lost horse, or to others of their kind. Be it what it may, almost every night the Mongols came loping into camp on their hardy, little ponies.

But this evening, when we had prepared an especial celebration, the audience did not arrive. It was a bitter disappointment, for we were consumed with curiosity to know what effect the blazing arc would have upon the Mongolian stoics. We could not believe that natives had not seen the light but probably they thought it was some spirit manifestation which was to be avoided. An hour after we were snuggled in our fur sleeping bags, two Mongols rode into camp, but we were too sleepy to give an exhibition of the fireworks.

We reached Panj-kiang about noon of the second day and found that a large mud house and a spacious compound had been erected beside the telegraph station by the Chinese company which was endeavoring to maintain a passenger service between Kalgan and Urga. The Chinese government also had invaded the field and was sending automobiles regularly to the Mongolian capital as a branch service of the Peking-Suiyuan railroad. In the previous September we had passed half a dozen of their motors in charge of a foreign representative of Messrs. Jardine, Matheson and Co. of Shanghai from whom the cars were purchased. He discovered immediately that the difficulties which the Chinese had encountered were largely the result of incompetent chauffeurs.

We had kept a sharp lookout for antelope, but saw nothing except a fox which looked so huge in the clear

air that all of us were certain it was a wolf. There
are always antelope on the Panj-kiang plain, however,
and we loaded the magazines of our rifles as soon as
we left the telegraph station. I was having a bit of
sport with an immense flock of golden plover (*Pluvialis
dominicus fulvus*) when the people in the cars signaled
me to return, for a fine antelope buck was standing
only a few hundred yards from the road. The ground
was as smooth and hard as an asphalt pavement and
we skimmed along at forty miles an hour. When the
animal had definitely made up its mind to cross in front
of us, Charles gave the accelerator a real push and the
car jumped to a speed of forty-eight miles. The antelope was doing his level best to "cross our bows" but
he was too far away, and for a few moments it seemed
that we would surely crash into him if he held his course.
It was a great race. Yvette had a death grip on my
coat, for I was sitting half over the edge of the car
ready to jump when Charles threw on the brakes.
With any one but Coltman at the wheel I would have
been too nervous to enjoy the ride, but we all had confidence in his superb driving.

The buck crossed the road not forty yards in front
of us, just at the summit of a tiny hill. Charles and
I both fired once, and the antelope turned half over in
a whirl of dust. It disappeared behind the hill crest
and we expected to find it dead on the other side, but
the slope was empty and even with our glasses we could
not discover a sign of life on the plain, which stretched
away to the horizon apparently as level as a floor. It

had been swallowed utterly as though by the magic pocket of a conjurer.

Mac had not participated in the fun, for it had been a one-man race. Fifteen minutes later, however, we had a "free for all" which gave him his initiation.

An extract from Yvette's "Journal" gives her impression of the chase:

"Some one pointed out the distant, moving specks on the horizon and in a moment our car had left the road and started over the plains. Nearer and nearer we came, and faster and faster ran the antelope stringing out in a long, yellow line before us. The speedometer was moving up and up, thirty miles, thirty-five miles. Roy was sitting on the edge of the car with his legs hanging out, rifle in hand, ready to swing to the ground as soon as the car halted. Mr. Coltman, who was driving, had already thrown on the brakes, but Roy, thinking in his excitement that he had stopped, jumped—and jumped too soon. The speed at which we were going threw him violently to the ground. I hardly dared look to see what had happened but somehow he turned a complete somersault, landed on his knees, and instantly began shooting. Mr. Coltman, his hands trembling with the exertion of the drive, opened fire across the wind shield. As the first reports crashed out, the antelope, which had seemed to be flying before, flattened out and literally skimmed over the plain. Half a dozen bullets struck behind the herd, then as Roy's rifle cracked again, one of those tiny specks dropped to the ground.

"It was a wonderful shot—four hundred and twenty yards measured distance.   No, this isn't a woman's inaccuracy of figures, it's a fact.   But then you must remember the extraordinary clearness of the air in Mongolia, where every object appears to be magnified half a dozen times.   The brilliant atmosphere is one of the most bewildering things of the desert.   Once we thought we saw an antelope grazing on the hillside and Mr. Coltman remarked disdainfully: 'Pooh, that's a horse.'   But the laugh was on him for as we drew near the 'horse' proved to be only a bleached bone.   At a short distance camels and ponies stood out as though cut in steel, seeming as high as a village church steeple; and, most ridiculous of all, my husband mistook me once at a long, long distance for a telegraph pole! Tartarin de Tarascon would have had some wonderful stories to tell of Mongolia!"

We had hardly reached the road again before Mrs. Coltman discovered a great herd of antelope on the slope of a low hill, and when the cars carried us over the crest we could see animals in every direction, feeding in pairs or in groups of ten to forty.

We all agreed that no better place could be found at which to obtain motion pictures and camp was made forthwith.   Unfortunately, the gazelles were shedding their winter coats and the skins were useless except for study; however, I did need half a dozen skeletons, so the animals we killed would not be wasted.

It was four o'clock in the afternoon when the tents were up and too late to take pictures; therefore, the photography was postponed until the next day, and we ran over toward a herd of antelope which was just visible on the sky line. When each of us had killed an animal, the opinion was unanimous that we had enough. I got mine on the first chase and thenceforth employed my time in making observations on the antelope's speed.

Time after time the car reached forty miles an hour, but with an even start the gazelles could swing about in front and "cross our bows." One of the antelope had a front leg broken just below the knee, and gave us a hard chase with the car going at thirty-five miles an hour. I estimated that even in its crippled condition the animal was traveling at a rate of *not less than twenty-five miles an hour*.

My field notes tell of a similar experience with the last gazelle which Mac killed late in the afternoon. ". . . We ran toward another group of antelope standing on the summit of a long land swell. There were fourteen in this herd and as the car neared them they trotted about with heads up, evidently trying to decide what species of plains animal we represented. The sun had just set, and I shall never forget the picture which they made, their graceful figures showing in black silhouettes against the rose glow of the evening sky. There was one buck among them and they seemed very nervous. When the men leaped out to shoot we were fully two hundred and fifty yards away, but at his third shot Mac dropped the buck. It was up again and off before the motor started in pursuit and, although running apart from the herd, it was only a short distance behind the others. Evidently the right foreleg was broken but with the car traveling at twenty-five miles an hour it was still drawing ahead. The going was not good and we ran for two miles without gaining an inch; then we came to a bit of smooth plain and the motor shot ahead at thirty-five miles an hour. We gained slowly and, when about one hundred yards away, I leaped out and fired at the animal breaking the other foreleg low down on the left side. Even with two legs injured it still traveled at a rate of fifteen miles, and a third shot was required to finish the unfortunate business. We found that both limbs were broken below the knee, and that the animal had been running on the stumps."

CHAPTER V

ANTELOPE MOVIE STARS

It was eight o'clock before we finished breakfast in the morning, but we did not wish to begin the motion picture photography until the sun was high enough above the horizon to give us a clear field for work. Charles and I rigged the tripod firmly in the *tonneau* of one of the cars. Mrs. Mac and Wang, a Chinese driver, were in the front seat, while Yvette and I squeezed in beside the camera. The Coltmans, Mac, and Owen occupied the other motor. We found a herd of antelope within a mile of camp and they paraded in beautiful formation as the car approached. It would have made a splendid picture, but although the two automobiles were of the same make, there was a vast difference in their speed and it was soon evident that we could not keep pace with the other motor. After two or three ineffectual attempts we roped the camera in the most powerful car, the three men came in with me, and the women transferred to Wang's machine.

The last herd of antelope had disappeared over a long hill, and when we reached the summit we saw that they had separated into four groups and scattered about on the plains below us. We selected the largest, con-

taining about fifty animals, and ran toward it as fast
as the car could travel. The herd divided when we
were still several hundred yards away, but the larger
part gave promise of swinging across our path. The
ground was thinly covered with short bunch grass, and
when we reached a speed of thirty-five miles an hour
the car was bounding and leaping over the tussocks
like a ship in a heavy gale. I tried to stand, but after
twice being almost pitched out bodily I gave it up and
operated the camera by kneeling on the rear seat.
Mac helped anchor me by sitting on my left leg, and
we got one hundred feet of film from the first herd.
Races with three other groups gave us two hundred
feet more, and as the gasoline in our tank was alarm-
ingly depleted we turned back toward camp.

Unfortunately I did not reload the camera with a
fresh roll of film and thereby missed one of the most
unusual and interesting pictures which ever could be
obtained upon the plains. The tents were already in
sight when a wolf suddenly appeared on the crest of
a grassy knoll. He looked at us for a moment and
then set off at an easy lope. The temptation was too
great to be resisted even though there was a strong
possibility that we might be stalled in the desert with
no gas.

The ground was smooth and hard, and our speedometer showed forty miles an hour. We soon began
to gain, but for three miles he gave us a splendid race.
Suddenly, as we came over a low hill, we saw an enormous herd of antelope directly in front of us. They

were not more than two hundred yards away, and the wolf made straight for them. Panic-stricken at the sight of their hereditary enemy followed by the roaring car, they scattered wildly and then swung about to cross our path. The wolf dashed into their midst and the herd divided as though cut by a knife. Some turned short about, but the others kept on toward us until I thought we would actually run them down. When not more than fifty yards from the motor they wheeled sharply and raced along beside the wolf.

To add to the excitement a fat, yellow marmot, which seemed suddenly to have lost his mind, galloped over the plain as fast as his short legs could carry him until he remembered that safety lay underground; then he popped into his burrow like a billiard ball into a pocket. With this strange assortment fleeing in front of the car we felt as though we had invaded a zoölogical garden.

The wolf paid not the slightest attention to the antelope for he had troubles of his own. We were almost on him, and I could see his red tongue between the foam-flecked jaws. Suddenly he dodged at right angles, and it was only by a clever bit of driving that Charles avoided crashing into him with the left front wheel. Before we could swing about the wolf had gained five hundred yards, but he was almost done. In another mile we had him right beside the car, and Coltman leaned far out to kill him with his pistol. The first bullet struck so close behind the animal that it turned him half over, and he dodged again just in time to meet a shot from Mac's rifle which broke his back. With its dripping lips drawn over a set of ugly teeth, the beast glared at us, as much as to say, "It is your move next, but don't come too close." Had it been any animal except a wolf I should have felt a twinge of pity, but I had no sympathy for the skulking brute. There will be more antelope next year because of its death.

All this had happened with an unloaded camera in the automobile. I had tried desperately to adjust a new roll of film, but had given up in despair for it was difficult enough even to sit in the bounding car. Were I to spend the remainder of my life in Mongolia there might never be such a chance again.

But we had an opportunity to learn just how fast a wolf can run, for the one we had killed was undoubtedly putting his best foot forward. I estimated that even at first he was not doing more than thirty-five miles an hour, and later we substantiated it on another, which gave us a race of twelve miles. With antelope which can reach fifty-five to sixty miles an hour a wolf has little chance, unless he catches them unawares, or finds the newly born young. To avoid just this the antelope are careful to stay well out on the plains where there are no rocks or hills to conceal a skulking wolf.

The wolf we had killed was shedding its hair and presented a most dilapidated, moth-eaten appearance; moreover, it had just been feeding on the carcass of a dead camel, which subsequently we discovered a mile away. When we reached camp I directed the two taxidermists to prepare the skeleton of the wolf, but to keep well away from the tents.

Charles and I had been talking a good deal about antelope steak, and for tiffin I had cut the fillets from one of the young gazelle. We were very anxious to "make good" on all that had been promised, so we cooked the steak ourselves. Just when the party was assembled in the tent for luncheon the Chinese began work upon the wolf. They had obediently gone to a considerable distance to perform the last rites, but had not chosen wisely in regard to the wind. As the antelope steak was brought in, a gentle breeze wafted with it a concentrated essence of defunct camel. Yvette put down her knife and fork and looked up. She caught my eye and burst out laughing. Mrs. Mac had her hand clasped firmly over her mouth and on her face was an expression of horror and deathly nausea.

Although I am a great lover of antelope steak, I will admit that when accompanied by *parfum de chameau*, especially when it is a very dead *chameau*, there are other things more attractive. Moreover, the antelope which we killed on the Panj-kiang plain really were very strong indeed. I have never been able to discover what was the cause, for those farther to the north were as delicious as any we have ever eaten. The introduction was such an unfortunate one that the party shied badly whenever antelope meat was mentioned during the remainder of the trip to Urga. Coltman, who had charge of the commissary, quite naturally expected that we would depend largely on meat and had not provided a sufficiency of other food. As a result we found that after the third day rations were becoming very short.

We camped that night at a well in a sandy river bottom about ten miles beyond Ude, the halfway point on the trip to Urga. It had been a bad day, with a bitterly cold wind which drove the dust and tiny pebbles against our faces like a continual storm of hail. As soon as the cars had stopped every one of us set to work with soap and water before anything had been done toward making camp. Our one desire was to remove a part of the dirt which had sifted into our eyes, hair, mouths, and ears. In half an hour we looked more brightly upon the world and began to wonder what we would have for dinner. It was a discussion which could not be carried on for very long since the bread was almost gone and only macaroni remained. Just then a demoiselle crane alighted beside the well not forty yards away. "There's our dinner," Charles shouted, "shoot it."

Two minutes later I was stripping off the feathers, and in less than five minutes it was sizzling in the pan. That was a bit too much for Mrs. Mac, hungry as she was. "Just think," she said, "that bird was walking about here not ten minutes ago and now it's on my plate. It hasn't stopped wiggling yet. I can't eat it!"

Poor girl, she went to bed hungry, and in the night waked to find her face terribly swollen from wind and sunburn. She was certain that she was about to die, but decided, like the "good sport" she is, to die alone upon the hillside where she wouldn't disturb the camp. After half an hour of wandering about she felt better, and returned to her sleeping bag on the sandy river bottom.

Just before dark we heard the *dong, dong, dong* of a camel's bell and saw the long line of dusty yellow animals swing around a sharp earth-corner into the sandy space beside the well. Like the trained units of an army each camel came into position, kneeled upon the ground and remained quietly chewing its cud until the driver removed the load. Long before the last straggler had arrived the tents were up and a fire blazing, and far into the night the thirsty beasts grunted and roared as the trough was filled with water.

For thirty-six days they had been on the road, and yet were only halfway across the desert. Every day had been exactly like the day before—an endless routine of eating and sleeping, camp-making and camp-breaking in sun, rain, or wind. The monotony of it all would be appalling to a westerner, but the Oriental mind seems peculiarly adapted to accept it with entire contentment. Long before daylight they were on the road again, and when we awoke only the smoking embers of an *argul* fire remained as evidence that they ever had been there.

Mongolia, as we saw it in the spring, was very different from Mongolia of the early autumn. The hills and plains stretched away in limitless waves of brown untinged by the slightest trace of green, and in shaded corners among rocks there were still patches of snow or ice. Instead of resembling the grassy plains of Kansas or Nebraska, now it was like a real desert and I had difficulty in justifying to Yvette and Mac my glowing accounts of its potential resources.

Moreover, the human life was just as disappointing as the lack of vegetation, for we were "between seasons" on the trail. The winter traffic was almost ended, and the camels would not be replaced by cart caravans until the grass was long enough to provide adequate food for oxen and horses. The *yurts,* which often are erected far out upon the plains away from water when snow is on the ground, had all been moved near the wells or to the summer pastures; and sometimes we traveled a hundred miles without a glimpse of even a solitary Mongol.

Ude had been left far behind, and we were bowling along on a road as level as a floor, when we saw two wolves quietly watching us half a mile away. We had agreed not to chase antelope again; but wolves were fair game at any time. Moreover, we were particularly glad to be able to check our records as to how fast a wolf can run when conditions are in its favor. Coltman signaled Mac to await us with the others, and we swung toward the animals which were trotting slowly westward, now and then stopping to look back as though reluctant to leave such an unusual exhibition as the car was giving them. A few moments later, however, they decided that curiosity might prove dangerous and began to run in earnest.

They separated almost immediately, and we raced

after the larger of the two, a huge fellow with rangy legs which carried him forward in a long, swinging lope. The ground was perfect for the car, and the speedometer registered forty miles an hour. He had a thousand-yard start, but we gained rapidly, and I estimated that he never reached a greater speed than thirty miles an hour. Charles was very anxious to kill the brute from the motor with his .45 caliber automatic pistol, and I promised not to shoot.

The wolf was running low to the ground, his head a little to one side watching us with one bloodshot eye. He was giving us a great race, but the odds were all against him, and finally we had him right beside the motor. Leaning far out, Coltman fired quickly. The bullet struck just behind the brute, and he swerved sharply, missing the right front wheel by a scant six inches. Before Charles could turn the car he had gained three hundred yards, but we reached him again in little more than a mile. As Coltman was about to shoot a second time, the wolf suddenly dropped from sight. Almost on the instant the car plunged over a bank four feet in height, landed with a tremendous shock—and kept on! Charles had seen the danger in a flash, and had thrown his body against the wheel to hold it steady. Had he not been an expert driver we should inevitably have turned upside down and probably all would have been killed.

We stopped an instant to inspect the springs, but by a miracle not a leaf was broken. The wolf halted, too, and we could see him standing on a gentle rise with drooping head, his gray sides heaving. He seemed to be "all in," but to our amazement he was off again like the wind even before the car had started. During the last three miles the ground had been changing rapidly, and we soon reached a stony plain where there was imminent danger of smashing a front wheel. The wolf was heading directly toward a rocky slope which lay against the sky like the spiny back of some gigantic monster of the past.

His strategy had almost won the race. For a moment the wolf rested on the ridge, and I leaped out to shoot, but instantly he dropped behind the bowlders. Leaving me to intercept the animal, Charles swung behind the ridge only to run at full speed into a sandy pocket. The motor ceased to throb, and the race was ended.

These wolves are sneaking carrion-feeders and as such I detest them, but this one had "played the game." *For twelve long miles* he had kept doggedly at his work without a whimper or a cry of "kamerad." The brute had outgeneraled us completely, had won by strategy and magnificent endurance. Whatever he supposed the roaring car to be, instinct told him that safety lay among the rocks and he led us there as straight as an arrow's flight.

The animal seemed to take an almost human enjoyment in the way we had been tricked, for he stood on a hillside half a mile away watching our efforts to extricate the car. We were in a bad place, and it was evident that the only method of escape was to remove all the baggage which was tied to the running boards. Spreading our fur sleeping bags upon the sand, we pushed and lifted the automobile to firm ground after an hour of strenuous work. Hardly had we started back to the road, when Charles suddenly clapped both hands to his face yelling, "My Lord, I'm burning up. What is it? I'm all on fire."

Mrs. Coltman pulled his hands away, revealing his face covered with blotches and rising blisters. At the same moment Yvette and I felt a shower of liquid fire stinging our hands and necks. We leaped out of the car just as another blast swept back upon us. Then Charles shouted, "I know. It's the Delco plant," and dived toward the front mud guard. Sure enough, the cover had been displaced from one of the batteries, and little pools of sulphuric acid had formed on the leather casings. The wind was blowing half a gale, and each gust showered us with drops of colorless liquid which bit like tiny, living coals.

In less than ten seconds I had slashed the ropes and the batteries were lying on the ground, but the acid had already done its work most thoroughly. The duffle sacks containing all our field clothes had received a liberal dose, and during the summer Yvette was kept busy patching shirts and trousers. I never would have believed that a little acid could go so far. Even garments in the very center of the sacks would suddenly disintegrate when we put them on, and the Hutukhtu and his electric plant were "blessed" many times before we left Mongolia.

When we reached the road, Mrs. Mac was sitting disconsolately in a car beside the servants. We had been gone nearly three hours and the poor girl was frantic with anxiety. Mac and Owen had followed our tracks in another motor, and arrived thirty minutes later. Mac's happy face was drawn and white.

"I wouldn't go through that experience again for all the money in Mongolia," he said. "We followed your tracks and at every hill expected to find you dead on the other side and the car upside down. How on earth did you miss capsizing when you went over that bank?"

At Turin we found Mr. and Mrs. Mamen camped near the telegraph station awaiting our arrival. The first cry was "Food! Food!" and two loaves of Russian bread which they had brought from Urga vanished in less than fifteen minutes. After taking several hundred feet of "movie" film at the monastery, we ran on northward over a road which was as smooth and hard as a billiard table. The Turin plain was alive with game; marmots, antelope, hares, bustards, geese, and cranes seemed to have concentrated there as though in a vast zoölogical garden, and we had some splendid shooting. But as Yvette and I spent two glorious months on this same plain, I will tell in future chapters how, in long morning horseback rides and during silent starlit nights, we learned to know and love it.

CHAPTER VI

THE SACRED CITY OF THE LIVING BUDDHA

Far up in northern Mongolia, where the forests stretch in an unbroken line to the Siberian frontier, lies Urga, the Sacred City of the Living Buddha. The world has other sacred cities, but none like this. It is a relic of medieval times overlaid with a veneer of twentieth-century civilization; a city of violent contrasts and glaring anachronisms. Motor cars pass camel caravans fresh from the vast, lone spaces of the Gobi Desert; holy lamas, in robes of flaming red or brilliant yellow, walk side by side with black-gowned priests; and swarthy Mongol women, in the fantastic headdress of their race, stare wonderingly at the latest fashions of their Russian sisters.

We came to Urga from the south. All day we had been riding over rolling, treeless uplands, and late in the afternoon we had halted on the summit of a hill overlooking the Tola River valley. Fifteen miles away lay Urga, asleep in the darkening shadow of the Bogdo-ol (God's Mountain). An hour later the road led us to our first surprise in Mai-ma-cheng, the Chinese quarter of the city. Years of wandering in the strange corners of the world had left us totally unprepared for what we saw. It seemed that here in Mongolia we had discovered an American frontier outpost of the Indian fighting days. Every house and shop was protected by high stockades of unpeeled timbers, and there was hardly a trace of Oriental architecture save where a temple roof gleamed above the palisades.

Before we were able to adjust our mental perspective we had passed from colonial America into a hamlet of modern Russia. Gayly painted cottages lined the road, and, unconsciously, I looked for a white church with gilded cupolas. The church was not in sight, but its place was taken by a huge red building of surpassing ugliness, the Russian Consulate. It stands alone on the summit of a knoll, the open plains stretching away behind it to the somber masses of the northern forests. In its imposing proportions it is tangible evidence of the Russian Colossus which not many years ago dominated Urga and all that is left of the ancient empire of the Khans.

For two miles the road is bordered by Russian cottages; then it debouches into a wide square which loses its distinctive character and becomes an indescribable mixture of Russia, Mongolia, and China. Palisaded compounds, gay with fluttering prayer flags, ornate houses, felt-covered *yurts,* and Chinese shops mingle in a dizzying chaos of conflicting personalities. Three great races have met in Urga and each carries on, in this far corner of Mongolia, its own customs and way of life. The Mongol *yurt* has remained unchanged; the Chinese shop, with its wooden counter and blue-gowned inmates, is pure Chinese; and the ornate cottages proclaim themselves to be only Russian.

But on the street my wife and I could never forget that we were in Mongolia. We never tired of wandering through the narrow alleys, with their tiny native shops, or of watching the ever-changing crowds. Mongols in half a dozen different tribal dresses, Tibetan pilgrims, Manchu Tartars, or camel drivers from far Turkestan drank and ate and gambled with Chinese from civilized Peking.

The barbaric splendor of the native dress fairly makes one gasp for breath. Besides gowns and sashes of dazzling brilliance, the men wear on their heads all the types of covering one learned to know in the pictures of ancient Cathay, from the high-peaked hat of yellow and black—through the whole, strange gamut—to the helmet with streaming peacock plumes. But were I to tell about them all I would leave none of my poor descriptive phrases for the women.

It is hopeless to draw a word-picture of a Mongol woman. A photograph will help, but to be appreciated she must be seen in all her colors. To begin with the dressing of her hair. If all the women of the Orient competed to produce a strange and fantastic type, I do not believe that they could excel what the Mongol matrons have developed by themselves.

Their hair is plaited over a frame into two enormous flat bands, curved like the horns of a mountain sheep and reënforced with bars of wood or silver. Each horn ends in a silver plaque, studded with bits of colored glass or stone, and supports a pendent braid like a riding quirt. On her head, between the horns, she wears a silver cap elaborately chased and flashing with "jewels." Surmounting this is a "saucer" hat of black and yellow. Her skirt is of gorgeous brocade or cloth, and the jacket is of like material with prominent "puffs" upon the shoulders. She wears huge leather boots with upturned, pointed toes, similar to those of the men, and when in full array she has a whole portiere of beadwork suspended from the region of her ears.

She is altogether satisfying to the lover of fantastic Oriental costumes, except in the matter of footgear, and this slight exception might be allowed, for she has so amply decorated every other available part of her anatomy.

Moreover, the boots form a very necessary adjunct to her personal equipment, besides providing a covering for her feet. They are many sizes too large, of course, but they furnish ample space during the bitter cold of winter for the addition of several pairs of socks, varying in number according to the thermometer. During the summer she often wears no socks at all, but their place is taken by an assortment of small articles which cannot be carried conveniently on her person. Her pipe and tobacco, a package of tea, or a wooden bowl can easily be stuffed into the wide top boots, for pockets are an unknown luxury even to the men.

In its kaleidoscopic mass of life and color the city is like a great pageant on the stage of a theater, with the added fascination of reality. But, somehow, I could

never quite make myself believe that it *was* real when a
brilliant group of horsemen in pointed, yellow hats and
streaming, peacock feathers dashed down the street. It
seemed too impossible that I, a wandering naturalist of
the drab, prosaic twentieth century, and my American
wife were really a living, breathing part of this strange
drama of the Orient.

But there was one point of contact which we had with
this dream-life of the Middle Ages. Yvette and I both
love horses, and the way to a Mongol's heart is through
his pony. Once on horseback we began to identify ourselves with the fascinating life around us. We lost the
uncomfortable sense of being merely spectators in the
Urga theatricals, and forgot that we had come to the
holy city by means of a very unromantic motor car.

We remained at Urga for ten days while preparations
were under way for our first trip to the plains, and returned to it often during the summer. We came to
know it well, and each time we rode down the long street
it seemed more wonderful that, in these days of com-
merce, Urga, and in fact all Mongolia, could have ex-
isted throughout the centuries with so little change.

There is, of course, no lack of modern influence in the
sacred city, but as yet it is merely a veneer which has
been lightly superimposed upon its ancient civilization,
leaving almost untouched the basic customs of its people. This has been due to the remoteness of Mongolia.
Until a few years ago, when motor cars first made their
way across the seven hundred miles of plains, the only
access from the south was by camel caravan, and the

monotonous trip offered little inducement to casual travelers. The Russians came to Urga from the north and, until the recent war, their influence was paramount along the border. They were by no means anxious to have other foreigners exploit Mongolia, and they wished especially to keep the country as a buffer-state between themselves and China.

Not only is Urga the capital of Mongolia and the only city of considerable size in the entire country but it is also the residence of the Hutukhtu, or Living Buddha, the head of both the Church and the State. Across the valley his palaces nestle close against the base of the Bogdo-ol (God's Mountain), which rises in wooded slopes from the river to an elevation of eleven thousand feet above sea level.

The Sacred Mountain is a vast game preserve, which is patrolled by two thousand lamas, and every approach is guarded by a temple or a camp of priests. Great herds of elk, roebuck, boar, and other animals roam the forests, but to shoot within the sacred precincts would mean almost certain death for the transgressor. Some years ago several Russians from Urga made their way up the mountain during the night and killed a bear. They were brought back in chains by a mob of frenzied lamas. Although the hunters had been beaten nearly to death, it required all the influence of the Russian diplomatic agent to save what remained of their lives.

The Bogdo-ol extends for twenty-five miles along the Tola Valley, shutting off Urga from the rolling plains to the south. Like a gigantic guardian of the holy city at its base, it stands as the only obstacle to the wireless station which is soon to be erected.

The Hutukhtu has three palaces on the banks of the Tola River. One of them is a hideous thing, built in Russian style. The other two at least have the virtue of native architecture. In the main palace the central structure is white with gilded cupolas, and smaller pavilions at the side have roofs of green. The whole is surrounded by an eight-foot stockade of white posts trimmed with red.

The Hutukhtu seldom leaves his palace now, for he is old and sick and almost blind. Many strange stories are told of the mysterious "Living God" which tend to show him "as of the earth earthy." It is said that in former days he sometimes left his "heaven" to revel with convivial foreigners in Urga; but all this is gossip and we are discussing a very saintly person. His passion for Occidental trinkets and inventions is well known, however, and his palace is a veritable storehouse for gramophones, typewriters, microscopes, sewing machines, and a host of other things sold to him by Russian traders and illustrated in picture catalogues sent from the uttermost corners of the world. But like a child he soon tires of his toys and throws them aside. He has a motor car, but he never rides in it. It has been reported that his chief use for the automobile is to attach a wire to its batteries and give his ministers an electric shock; for all Mongols love a practical joke, and the Hutukhtu is no exception.

Now his palace is wired for electricity, and a great arc

light illuminates the courtyard. One evening Mr. Lucander and Mr. Mamen, who sold the electric plant to
the Hutukhtu, were summoned to the palace to receive
payment. They witnessed a scene which to-day could
be possible only in Mongolia. Several thousand dollars
in silver were brought outside to their motor car, and
the lama, who paid the bills, insisted that they count it in
his presence.

A great crowd of Mongols had gathered near the palace and at last a long rope was let out from one of the
buildings. Kneeling, the Mongols reverently touched
the rope, which was gently waggled from the other end,
supposedly by the Hutukhtu. A barbaric monotone of
chanted prayers arose from the kneeling suppliants, and
the rope was waggled again. Then the Mongols rode
away, silent with awe at having been blessed by the
Living God. All this under a blazing electric light beside an automobile at the foot of the Bogdo-ol!

The Hutukhtu seemed to feel that it became his station as a ruling monarch to have a foreign house with
foreign furniture. Of course he never intended to live
in it, but other kings had useless palaces and why
shouldn't he? Therefore, a Russian atrocity of red brick
was erected a half mile or so from his other dwellings.
The furnishing became a matter of moment, and Mr.
Lucander, who was temporarily in the employ of the
Mongolian Government, was intrusted with the task of
attending to the intimate details. The selection of a
bed was most important, for even Living Buddhas have
to sleep sometimes—they cannot always be blessing

adoring subjects or playing jokes on their ministers of
state. With considerable difficulty a foreign bed was
purchased and brought across the seven hundred miles
of plains and desert to the red brick palace on the banks
of the Tola River.

Mr. Lucander superintended its installation in the
Hutukhtu's boudoir and himself turned chambermaid.
As this was the first time he had ever made a bed for a
Living God, he arranged the spotless sheets and turned
down the covers with the greatest care. When all was
done to his satisfaction he reported to one of the Hutukhtu's ministers that the bed was ready. Two lamas,
high dignitaries of the church, were the inspection com-
mittee. They agreed that it *looked* all right, but the
question was, how did it *feel?* Mr. Lucander waxed eloquent on the "springiness" of the springs, and assured
them that no bed could be better; that this was the bed
par excellence of all the beds in China. The lamas held
a guttural consultation and then announced that before
the bed could be accepted it must be tested. Therefore,
without more ado, each lama in his dirty boots and gown
laid his unwashed self upon the bed, and bounced up
and down. The result was satisfactory—except to Lucander and the sheets.

Although to foreign eyes and in the cold light of
modernity the Hutukhtu and his government cut a somewhat ridiculous figure, the reverse of the picture is the
pathetic death struggle of a once glorious race. I have
said that unaccustomed luxury was responsible for the
decline of the Mongol Empire, but the ruin of the race

was due to the Lama Church. Lamaism, which was introduced from Tibet, gained its hold not long after the time of Kublai Khan's death in 1295. Previous to this the Mongols had been religious liberals, but eventually Lamaism was made the religion of the state. It is a branch of the Buddhist cult, and its teachings are against war and violent death.

By custom one or more sons of every family are dedicated to the priesthood, and as Lamaism requires its priests to be celibate, the birth rate is low. To-day there are only a few million Mongols in a country half as large as the United States (exclusive of Alaska), a great proportion of the male population being lamas. With no education, except in the books of their sect, they lead a lazy, worthless existence, supported by the lay population and by the money they extract by preying upon the superstitions of their childlike brothers. Were Lamaism abolished there still would be hope for Mongolia under a proper government, for the Mongols of to-day are probably the equals of Genghis Khan's warriors in strength, endurance, and virility.

The religion of Mongolia is like that of Tibet and the Dalai Lama of Lhassa is the head of the entire Church. The Tashi Lama residing at Tashilumpo, also in Tibet, ranks second. The Hutukhtu of Mongolia is third in the Lama hierarchy, bearing the title *Cheptsundampa Hutukhtu* (Venerable Best Saint). According to ancient tradition, the Hutukhtu never dies; his spirit simply reappears in the person of some newly born infant and thus comes forth reëmbodied. The names of infants, who have been selected as possible candidates for the honor, are written upon slips of paper incased in rolls of paste and deposited in a golden urn. The one which is drawn is hailed as the new incarnation.

Some years ago the eyesight of the Hutukhtu began to fail, and a great temple was erected as a sacrifice to appease the gods. It stands on a hill at the western end of Urga, surrounded by the tiny wooden dwellings of the priests. "The Lama City" it is called, for only those in the service of the Church are allowed to live within its sacred precincts. In the temple itself there is an eighty-foot bronze image of Buddha standing on a golden lotus flower. The great figure is heavily gilded, incrusted with precious stones, and draped with silken cloths.

I was fortunate in being present one day when the temple was opened to women and the faithful in the city. Somewhat doubtful as to my reception, I followed the crowd as it filed through an outer pavilion between a double row of kneeling lamas in high-peaked hats and robes of flaming yellow. I carried my hat in my hand and tried to wear a becoming expression of humility and reverence. It was evidently successful, for I passed unhindered into the Presence. At the entrance stood a priest who gave me, with the others, a few drops of holy water from a filthy jug. Silent with awe, the people bathed their faces with the precious fluid and prostrated themselves before the gigantic figure standing on the golden lotus blossom, its head lost in the shadows of the temple roof. They kissed its silken draperies, soiled by the lips of other thousands, and each one gathered a handful of sacred dirt from the temple floor. From niches in the walls hundreds of tiny Buddhas gazed impassively on the worshiping Mongols.

The scene was intoxicating in its barbaric splendor. The women in their fantastic headdresses and brilliant gowns; the blazing yellow robes of the kneeling lamas; and the chorus of prayers which rose and fell in a meaningless half-wild chant broken by the clash of cymbals and the boom of drums—all this set the blood leaping in my veins. There was a strange dizziness in my head, and I had an almost overpowering desire to fall on my knees with the Mongols and join in the chorus of adoration. The subtle smell of burning incense, the brilliant colors, and the barbaric music were like an intoxicating drink which inflamed the senses but dulled the brain. It was then that I came nearest to understanding the religious fanaticism of the East. Even with a background of twentieth-century civilization I felt its sensuous power. What wonder that it has such a hold on a simple, uneducated people, fed on superstition from earliest childhood and the religious traditions of seven hundred years!

The service ended abruptly in a roar of sound. Rising to their feet, the people streamed into the courtyard to whirl the prayer wheels about the temple's base. Each wheel is a hollow cylinder of varying size, standing on end, and embellished with Tibetan characters in gold. The wheels are sometimes filled with thousands of slips of paper upon which is written a prayer or a sacred thought, and each revolution adds to the store of merit in the future life.

The Mongol goes farther still in accumulating virtue, and every native house in Urga is gay with fluttering bits of cloth or paper on which a prayer is written. Each time the little flag moves in the wind it sends forth a supplication for the welfare of the Mongol's spirit in the Buddhistic heaven. Not only are the prayer wheels found about the temples, but they line the streets, and no visiting Mongol need be deprived of trying the virtue of a new device without going to a place of worship. He can give a whirl or two to half a dozen within a hundred yards of where he buys his tea or sells his sheep.

On every hand there is constant evidence that Urga is a sacred city. It never can be forgotten even for a moment. The golden roofs of scores of temples give back the sunlight, and the moaning chant of praying lamas is always in the air. Even in the main street I have seen the prostrate forms of ragged pilgrims who have journeyed far to this Mecca of the lama faith. If they are entering the city for the first time and crave exceeding virtue, they approach the great temple on the hill by lying face down at every step and beating their foreheads upon the ground. Wooden shrines of dazzling whiteness stand in quiet streets or cluster by themselves behind the temples. In front of each, raised slightly at one end, is a prayer board worn black and smooth by the prostrated bodies of worshiping Mongols.

Although the natives take such care for the repose of the spirit in after life, they have a strong distaste for the body from which the spirit has fled and they consider it a most undesirable thing to have about the house. The stigma is imposed even upon the dying. In Urga a family of Mongols had erected their *yurt* in the court-yard of one of our friends. During the summer the young wife became very ill, and when her husband was convinced that she was about to die he moved the poor creature bodily out of the *yurt*. She could die if she wished, but it must not be inside his house.

The corpse itself is considered unclean and the abode of evil spirits, and as such must be disposed of as quickly as possible. Sometimes the whole family will pack up their *yurt* and decamp at once, leaving the body where it lies. More usually the corpse is loaded upon a cart which is driven at high speed over a bit of rough ground. The body drops off at some time during the journey, but the driver does not dare look back until he is sure that the unwelcome burden is no longer with him; otherwise he might anger the spirit following the corpse and thereby cause himself and his family unending trouble. Unlike the Chinese, who treat their dead with the greatest respect and go to enormous expense in the burial, every Mongol knows that his coffin will be the stomachs of dogs, wolves, or birds. Indeed, the Chinese name for the raven is the "Mongol's coffin."

The first day we camped in Urga, my wife and Mrs. MacCallie were walking beside the river. Only a short distance from our tent they discovered a dead Mongol who had just been dragged out of the city. A pack of dogs were in the midst of their feast and the sight was most unpleasant.

The dogs of Mongolia are savage almost beyond belief. They are huge black fellows like the Tibetan mastiff, and their diet of dead human flesh seems to have given them a contempt for living men. Every Mongol family has one or more, and it is exceedingly dangerous for a man to approach a *yurt* or caravan unless he is on horseback or has a pistol ready. In Urga itself you will probably be attacked if you walk unarmed through the meat market at night. I have never visited Constantinople, but if the Turkish city can boast of more dogs than Urga, it must be an exceedingly disagreeable place in which to dwell. Although the dogs live to a large extent upon human remains, they are also fed by the lamas. Every day about four o'clock in the afternoon you can see a cart being driven through the main street, followed by scores of yelping dogs. On it are two or more dirty lamas with a great barrel from which they ladle out refuse for the dogs, for according to their religious beliefs they accumulate great merit for themselves if they prolong the life of anything, be it bird, beast, or insect.

In the river valley, just below the Lama City, numbers of dogs can always be found, for the dead priests usually are thrown there to be devoured. Dozens of white skulls lie about in the grass, but it is a serious matter even to touch one. I very nearly got into trouble one day by targeting my rifle upon a skull which lay two or three hundred yards away from our tent.

The customs of the Mongols are not all as gruesome as those I have described, yet Urga is essentially a frontier city where life is seen in the raw. Its natives are a hard-living race, virile beyond compare. Children of the plains, they are accustomed to privation and fatigue. Their law is the law of the northland:

". . . . That only the Strong shall thrive,
That surely the Weak shall perish and only the Fit survive."

In the careless freedom of his magnificent horsemanship a Mongol seems as much an untamed creature of the plains as does the eagle itself which soars above his *yurt*. Independence breathes in every movement; even in his rough good humor and in the barbaric splendor of the native dress.

But the little matter of cleanliness is of no importance in his scheme of life. When a meal has been eaten, the wooden bowl is licked clean with the tongue; it is seldom washed. Every man and woman usually carries through life the bodily dirt which has accumulated in childhood, unless it is removed by some accident or by the wear of years. One can be morally certain that it will never be washed off by design or water. Perhaps the native is not altogether to blame, for, except in the north, water is not abundant. It can be found on the plains and in the Gobi Desert only at wells and an occasional pond, and on the march it is too precious to be wasted in the useless process of bathing. Moreover, from September until May the bitter winds which sweep down from the

Siberian steppes furnish an unpleasant temperature in which to take a bath.

The Mongol's food consists almost entirely of mutton, cheese, and tea. Like all northern people, he needs an abundance of fat, and sheep supply his wants. There is always more or less grease distributed about his clothes and person, and when Mongols are *en masse* the odor of mutton and unwashed humanity is well-nigh overpowering.

I must admit that in morality the Mongol is but little better off than in personal cleanliness. A man may have only one lawful wife, but may keep as many concubines as his means allow, all of whom live with the members of the family in the single room of the *yurt*. Adultery is openly practiced, apparently without prejudice to either party, and polyandry is not unusual in the more remote parts of the country.

The Mongol is *unmoral* rather than *immoral*. He lives like an untaught child of nature and the sense of modesty or decency, as we conceive it, does not enter into his scheme of life. But the operation of natural laws, which in the lower animals are successful in maintaining the species, is fatally impaired by the loose family relations which tend to spread disease. Unless Lamaism is abolished I can see little hope for the rejuvenation of the race.

In writing of Urga's inhabitants and their way of life I am neglecting the city itself. I have already told of the great temple on the hill and its clustering lama houses which overlook and dominate the river valley.

Its ornate roof, flashing in the sun, can be seen for many miles, like a religious beacon guiding the steps of wandering pilgrims to the Mecca of their faith.

At the near end of the broad street below the Lama City is the tent market, and just beyond it are the blacksmith shops where bridles, cooking pots, tent pegs, and all the equipment essential to a wandering life on the desert can be purchased in an hour—if you have the price! Nothing is cheap in Urga, with the exception of horses, and when we began to outfit for our trip on the plains we received a shock similar to that which I had a month ago in New York, when I paid twenty dollars for a pair of shoes. We ought to be hardened to it now, but when we were being robbed in Urga by profiteering Chinese, who sell flour at ten and twelve dollars a sack and condensed milk at seventy-five cents a tin, we roared and grumbled—and paid the price! I vowed I would never pay twenty dollars for a pair of shoes at home, but roaring and grumbling is no more effective in procuring shoes in New York than it was in obtaining flour and milk in Urga.

We paid in Russian rubles, then worth three cents each. (In former years a ruble equaled more than half a dollar.) Eggs were well-nigh nonexistent, except those which had made their way up from China over the long caravan trail and were guaranteed to be "addled" —or whatever it is that sometimes makes an egg an unpleasant companion at the breakfast table. Even those cost three rubles each! Only a few Russians own chickens in Urga and their productions are well-nigh "golden eggs," for grain is very scarce and it takes an astounding number of rubles to buy a bushel.

Fortunately we had sent most of our supplies and equipment to Urga by caravan during the winter, but there were a good many odds and ends needed to fill our last requirements, and we came to know the ins and outs of the sacred city intimately before we were ready to leave for the plains. The Chinese shops were our real help, for in Urga, as everywhere else in the Orient, the Chinese are the most successful merchants. Some firms have accumulated considerable wealth and the Chinaman does not hesitate to exact the last cent of profit when trading with the Mongols.

At the eastern end of Urga's central street, which is made picturesque by gayly painted prayer wheels and alive with a moving throng of brilliant horsemen, are the Custom House and the Ministry of Foreign Affairs. The former is at the far end of an enormous compound filled with camel caravans or loaded carts. There is a more or less useless wooden building, but the business is conducted in a large *yurt*, hard against the compound wall. It was an extraordinary contrast to see a modern filing-cabinet at one end and a telephone box on the felt-covered framework of the *yurt*.

Not far beyond the Custom House is what I believe to be one of the most horrible prisons in the world. Inside a double palisade of unpeeled timbers is a space about ten feet square upon which open the doors of small rooms, almost dark. In these dungeons are piled wooden boxes, four feet long by two and one-half feet high. These coffins are the prisoners' cells.

Some of the poor wretches have heavy chains about their necks and both hands manacled together. They can neither sit erect nor lie at full length. Their food, when the jailer remembers to give them any, is pushed through a six-inch hole in the coffin's side. Some are imprisoned here for only a few days or weeks; others for life, or for many years. Sometimes they lose the use of their limbs, which shrink and shrivel away. The agony of their cramped position is beyond the power of words to describe. Even in winter, when the temperature drops, as it sometimes does, to sixty degrees below zero, they are given only a single sheepskin for covering. How it is possible to live in indescribable filth, half-fed, well-nigh frozen in winter, and suffering the tortures of the damned, is beyond my ken—only a Mongol could live at all.

The prison is not a Mongol invention. It was built by the Manchus and is an eloquent tribute to a knowledge of the fine arts of cruelty that has never been surpassed.

I have given this description of the prison not to feed morbid curiosity, but to show that Urga, even if it has a Custom House, a Ministry of Foreign Affairs, motor cars, and telephones, is still at heart a city of the Middle Ages.

In Urga we made a delightful and most valuable friend in the person of Mr. F. A. Larsen. Most foreigners speak of him as "Larsen of Mongolia" and indeed it is difficult for us to think of the country without thinking of the man. Some thirty years ago he rode into Mongolia and liked it. He liked it so much, in fact, that he dug a well and built a house among the Tabool hills a hundred miles north of Kalgan. At first he labored with his wife as a missionary, but later he left that field to her and took up the work which he loved best in all the world—the buying and selling of horses.

During his years of residence in Mongolia hundreds of thousands of horses have passed under his appraising eyes and the Mongols respect his judgment as they respect the man. I wish that I might write the story of his life, for it is more interesting than any novel of romance or adventure. In almost every recent event of importance to the Mongols Mr. Larsen's name has figured. Time after time he has been sent as an emissary of the Living Buddha to Peking when misunderstandings or disturbances threatened the political peace of Mongolia. Not only does he understand the psychology of the natives, but he knows every hill and plain of their vast plateau as well as do the desert nomads.

For some time he had been in charge of Andersen, Meyer's branch at Urga with Mr. E. W. Olufsen and we made their house our headquarters. Mr. Larsen immediately undertook to obtain an outfit for our work upon the plains. He purchased two riding ponies for us from Prince Tze Tze; he borrowed two carts with harness from a Russian friend, and bought another; he loaned us a riding pony for our Mongol, a cart horse of his own, and Mr. Olufsen contributed another. He made our equipment a personal matter and he was never too busy to assist us in the smallest details. Moreover, we could spend hours listening to the tales of his early life, for his keen sense of humor made him a delightful story-teller. One of the most charming aspects of our wandering life is the friends we have made in far corners of the world, and for none have we a more affectionate regard than for "Larsen of Mongolia."

CHAPTER VII

THE LONG TRAIL TO SAIN NOIN KHAN

Our arrival in Urga was in the most approved manner of the twentieth century. We came in motor cars with much odor of gasoline and noise of horns. When we left the sacred city we dropped back seven hundred years and went as the Mongols traveled. Perhaps it was not quite as in the days of Genghis Khan, for we had three high-wheeled carts of a Russian model, but they were every bit as springless and uncomfortable as the palanquins of the ancient emperors.

Of course, we ourselves did not ride in carts. They were driven by our cook and the two Chinese taxidermists, each of whom sat on his own particular mound of baggage with an air of resignation and despondency. Their faces were very long indeed, for the sudden transition from the back seat of a motor car to a jolting cart did not harmonize with their preconceived scheme of Mongolian life. But they endured it manfully, and doubtless it added much to the store of harrowing experience with which they could regale future audiences in civilized Peking.

My wife and I were each mounted on a Mongol pony. Mine was called "Kublai Khan" and he deserved the name. Later I shall have much to tell of this wonderful horse, for I learned to love him as one loves a friend who has endured the "ordeal by fire" and has not been found wanting. My wife's chestnut stallion was a trifle smaller than Kublai Khan and proved to be a tricky beast whom I could have shot with pleasure. To this day she carries the marks of both his teeth and hoofs, and we have no interest in his future life. Kublai Khan has received the reward of a sunlit stable in Peking where carrots are in abundance and sugar is not unknown.

Besides the three Chinese we had a little Mongol priest, a yellow lama only eighteen years of age. We did not hire him for spiritual reasons, but to be our guide and social mentor upon the plains. Of course, we could not speak Mongol, but both my wife and I know some Chinese and our cook-boy Lü was possessed of a species of "pidgin English" which, by using a good deal of imagination, we could understand at times. Since our lama spoke fluent Chinese, he acted as interpreter with the Mongols, and we had no difficulty. It is wonderful how much you can do with sign language when you really have to, especially if the other fellow tries to understand. You always can be sure that the Mongols will match your efforts in this respect.

An interesting part of our equipment was a Mongol tent which Charles Coltman had had made for us in Kalgan. This is an ingenious adaptation of the ordinary wall tent, and is especially fitted for work on the plains. No one should attempt to use any other kind. From the ridgepole the sides curve down and out to the ground, presenting a sloping surface to the wind at every angle. One corner can be lifted to cause a draft through the door and an open fire can be built in the tent without danger of suffocation from the smoke; moreover, it can be erected by a single person in ten minutes. We had an American wall tent also, but found it such a nuisance that we used it only during bad weather. In the wind which always blows upon the plains it flapped and fluttered to such a degree that we could hardly sleep.

As every traveler knows, the natives of a country usually have developed the best possible clothes and dwellings for the peculiar conditions under which they live. Just as the Mongol felt-covered *yurt* and tent are all that can be desired, so do they know that fur and leather are the only clothing to keep them warm during the bitter winter months.

In the carts we had an ample supply of flour, bacon, coffee, tea, sugar, and dried fruit. For meat, we depended upon our guns, of course, and always had as much as could be used. Although we did not travel *de luxe,* nevertheless we were entirely comfortable. When a man boasts of the way in which he discards even necessaries in the field, you can be morally certain that he has not done much real traveling. "Roughing it" does not harmonize well with hard work. One must accept enough discomforts under the best conditions without the addition of any which can be avoided. Good health is the prime requisite in the field. Without it you are lost. The only way in which to keep fit and ready to give every ounce of physical and mental energy to the problems of the day is to sleep comfortably, eat wholesome food, and be properly clothed. It is not often, then, that you will need a doctor. We have not as yet had a physician on any of our expeditions, even though we have often been very many miles from the nearest white men.

It never ceases to amuse me that the insurance companies always cancel my accident policies as soon as I leave for the field. The excuse is that I am not a "good risk," although they are ready enough to renew them when I return to New York. And yet the average person has a hundred times more chance of being killed or injured right on Fifth Avenue than do we who live in the open, breathing God's fresh air and sleeping under the stars. My friend Stefansson, the Arctic explorer, often says that "adventures are a mark of incompetence," and he is doubtless right. If a man goes into the field with a knowledge of the country he is to visit and with a proper equipment, he probably will have very few "adventures." If he has not the knowledge and equipment he had much better remain at home, for he will inevitably come to grief.

We learned from the Mongols that there was a wonderful shooting ground three hundred miles southwest of Urga in the country belonging to Sain Noin Khan. It was a region backed by mountains fifteen thousand feet in height, inhabited by bighorn sheep and ibex; and antelope were reported to be numerous upon the plains which merged gradually into the sandy wastes of the western Gobi where herds of wild horses (*Equus prje-*

valski) and wild asses (*Equus hemionus*) could be found.

Sain Noin, one of the four Mongolian kings, had died only a short time earlier under suspicious circumstances, and his widow had just visited the capital. Monsieur Orlow, the Russian Diplomatic Agent, had written her regarding our prospective visit, and through him she had extended to us a cordial invitation.

Our start from Urga was on a particularly beautiful day, even for Mongolia. The golden roof of the great white temple on the hill blazed with light, and the undulating crest of the Sacred Mountain seemed so near that we imagined we could see the deer and boar in its parklike openings. Our way led across the valley and over the Tola River just below the palace of the Living God. We climbed a long hill and emerged on a sloping plain where marmots were bobbing in and out of their burrows like toy animals manipulated by a string. Two great flocks of demoiselle cranes were daintily catching grasshoppers not a hundred yards away. We wanted both the cranes for dinner and the marmots for specimens, but we dared not shoot. Although not actually upon sacred soil we were in close proximity to the Bogdo-ol and a rifle shot might have brought a horde of fanatical priests upon our heads. It is best to take no chances with religious superstitions, for the lamas do not wait to argue when they are once aroused.

The first day began most beautifully, but it ended badly as all first days are apt to do. We met our "Waterloo" on a steep hill shortly after tiffin, for two of the horses absolutely refused to pull. The loads were evidently too heavy, and the outlook for the future was not encouraging. An extract from my wife's journal tells what we did that afternoon.

"It took two hours to negotiate the hill, and the men were almost exhausted when the last load reached the summit. Ever since tiffin the sky had been growing darker and darker, and great masses of black clouds gathered about the crest of the Bogdo-ol. Suddenly a vivid flash of lightning cut the sky as though with a flaming knife, and the rain came down in a furious beat of icy water. In five minutes we were soaked and shivering with cold, so when at last we reached the plain we turned off the road toward two Mongol *yurts,* which rested beside the river a mile away like a pair of great white birds.

"Roy and I galloped ahead over the soft, slushy grass, nearly blinded by the rain, and hobbling our horses outside the nearest *yurt,* went inside with only the formality of a shout. The room was so dark that I could hardly see, and the heavy smoke from the open fire burned and stung our eyes. On the floor sat a frowzy-looking woman, blowing at the fire, and a yellow lama, his saucer hat hidden under its waterproof covering—apparently he was a traveler like ourselves.

"The frowzy lady smiled and motioned us to sit down on a low couch beside the door. As we did so, I saw a small face peering out of a big sheepskin coat and two black eyes staring at us unblinkingly. It was a little Mongol girl whose nap had been disturbed by so many visitors. She was rather a pretty little thing and so small—just a little older than my own baby in Peking —that I wanted to play with her. She was shy at first, but when I held out a picture advertisement from a package of cigarettes she gradually edged nearer, encouraged by her mother. Soon she was leaning on my knee. Then without taking her black eyes from my face, she solemnly put one finger in her mouth and jerked it out with a loud 'pop,' much to her mother's gratification. But when she decided to crawl up into my lap, my interest began to wane, for she exuded such a concentrated 'essence of Mongol' and rancid mutton fat that I was almost suffocated.

"Our hostess was busy stirring a thick, white soup in a huge caldron, and by the time the carts arrived every one was dipping in with their wooden bowls. We begged to be excused, since we had already had some experience with Mongol soup.

"The *yurt* really was not a bad place when we became accustomed to the bitter smoke and the combination of native odors. There were two couches, about six inches from the ground, covered with sheepskins and furs. Opposite the door stood a chest—rather a nice one—on top of which was a tiny god with a candle burning before it, and a photograph of the Hutukhtu."

We had dinner in the *yurt*, and the boys slept there while we used our Mongol tent. There was no difficulty in erecting it even in the wind and rain, but it would have been impossible to have put up the American wall tent. Even though it was the fifth of June, there was a sharp frost during the night, and we were thankful for our fur sleeping bags.

Always in Mongolia after a heavy rain the air is crystal-clear, and we had a delightful morning beside the river. Hundreds of demoiselle cranes were feeding in the meadowlike valley bottom where the grass was as green as emeralds. We saw two of the graceful birds standing on a sand bar and, as we rode toward them, they showed not the slightest sign of fear. When we were not more than twenty feet away they walked slowly about in a circle, and the lama discovered two spotted brown eggs almost under his pony's feet. There was no sign of a nest, but the eggs were perfectly protected by their resemblance to the stones.

Our way led close along the Tola River, and just before tiffin we saw a line of camels coming diagonally toward us from behind a distant hill. I wish you could have seen that caravan in all its barbaric splendor as it wound across the vivid green plains. Three lamas, dressed in gorgeous yellow robes, and two, in flaming red, rode ahead on ponies. Then neck and neck, mounted on enormous camels, came four men in gowns of rich maroon and a woman flashing with jewels and silver. Behind them, nose to tail, was the long, brown line of laden beasts. It was like a painting of the Middle Ages—like a picture of the days of Kublai Khan, when the Mongol court was the most splendid the world has ever seen. My wife and I were fascinated, for this was the Mongolia of our dreams.

But our second day was not destined to be one of un-
alloyed happiness, for just after luncheon we reached a
bad stretch of road alternating between jagged rocks
and deep mud holes. The white horse, which was so
quickly exhausted the day before, gave up absolutely
when its cart became badly mired. Just then a red
lama appeared with four led ponies and said that one of
his horses could extricate the cart. He hitched a tiny
brown animal between the shafts, we all put our shoulders to the wheels, and in ten minutes the load was on
solid ground. We at once offered to trade horses, and
by giving a bonus of five dollars I became the possessor
of the brown pony.

But the story does not end there. Two months later
when we had returned to Urga a Mongol came to our
camp in great excitement and announced that we had
one of his horses. He said that five animals had been
stolen from him and that the little brown pony for which
I had traded with the lama was one of them. His proof
was incontrovertible and according to the law of the
country I was bound to give back the animal and accept
the loss. However, a half dozen hard-riding Mongol
soldiers at once took up the trail of the lama, and the
chances are that there will be one less thieving priest
before the incident is closed.

It is interesting to note how a similarity of conditions
in western America and in Mongolia has developed
exactly the same attitude of mutual protection in regard
to horses. In both countries horse-stealing is considered
to be one of the worst crimes. It is punishable by death

in Mongolia or, what is infinitely worse, by a life in one
of the prison coffins. Moreover, the spirit of mutual
assistance is carried further, and several times during
the summer when our ponies had strayed miles from the
tents they were brought in by passing Mongols, or we
were told where they could be found.

Our camp the second night was on a beautiful, grassy
plateau beside a tiny stream, a tributary of the river.
We put out a line of traps for small mammals, but in the
morning were disappointed to find only three meadow
mice (*Microtus*). There were no fresh signs of marmots, hares, or other animals along the river, and I began to suspect what eventually proved to be true, viz.,
that the valley was a favorite winter camping ground
for Mongols, and that all the game had been killed or
driven far away. Indeed, we had hardly been beyond
sight of a *yurt* during the entire two days, and great
flocks of sheep and goats were feeding on every grassy
meadow.

But the Mongols considered cartridges too precious
to waste on birds and we saw many different species.
The demoiselle cranes were performing their mating
dances all about us, and while one was chasing a magpie
it made the most amusing spectacle, as it hopped and
flapped after the little black and white bird which kept
just out of reach.

Mongolian skylarks were continually jumping out of
the grass from almost under our horses' feet to soar
about our heads, flooding the air with song. Along the
sand banks of the river we saw many flocks of swan

geese (*Cygnopsis cygnoides*). They are splendid fellows with a broad, brown band down the back of the neck, and are especially interesting as being the ancestors of the Chinese domestic geese. They were not afraid of horses, but left immediately if a man on foot approached. I killed half a dozen by slipping off my pony, when about two hundred yards away, and walking behind the horses while Yvette rode boldly toward the flock, leading Kublai Khan. Twice the birds fell across the river, and we had to swim for them. My pony took to the water like a duck and when we had reached the other bank would arch his neck as proudly as though he had killed the bird himself. His keen interest in sport, his gentleness, and his intelligence won my heart at once. He would let me shoot from his back without the slightest fear, even though he had never been used as a hunting pony by Prince Tze Tze from whom he had been purchased.

In the ponds and among the long marsh grass we found the ruddy sheldrake (*Casarca casarca*), and the crested lapwing (*Vanellus vanellus*). They were like old friends, for we had met them first in far Yün-nan and on the Burma frontier during the winter of 1916-17 whence they had gone to escape the northern cold; now they were on their summer breeding grounds. The sheldrakes glowed like molten gold when the sun found them in the grass, and we could not have killed the beautiful birds even had we needed them for food. Moreover, like the lapwings, they had a trusting simplicity, a way of throwing themselves on one's mercy, which was in-

finitely appealing. We often hunted for the eggs of
both the sheldrakes and lapwings. They must have been
near by, we knew, for the old birds would fly about our
heads uttering agonizing calls, but we never found the
nests.

I killed four light-gray geese with yellow bills and
legs and narrow brown bars across the head, and a
broad brown stripe down the back of the neck. I could
only identify the species as the bar-headed goose of India (*Eulabeia indica*), which I was not aware ever traveled so far north to breed. Later I found my
identification to be correct, and that the bird is an occasional visitor to Mongolia. We saw only one specimen
of the bean goose (*Anser fabalis*), the common bird of
China, which I had expected would be there in thousands. There were a few mallards, redheads, and shoveler ducks, and several bustards, besides half a dozen
species of plover and shore birds.

Except for these the trip would have been infinitely
monotonous, for we were bitterly disappointed in the
lack of animal life. Moreover, there was continual
trouble with the carts, and on the third day I had to buy
an extra horse. Although one can purchase a riding
pony at any *yurt*, cart animals are not easy to find, for
the Mongols use oxen or camels to draw most loads.
The one we obtained had not been in the shafts for more
than two years and was badly frightened when we
brought him near the cart. It was a liberal education
to see our Mongol handle that horse! He first put a
hobble on all four legs, then he swung a rope about the

hind quarters, trussed him tightly, and swung him into the shafts. When the pony was properly harnessed, he fastened the bridle to the rear of the other cart and drove slowly ahead. At first the horse tried to kick and plunge, but the hobbles held him fast and in fifteen minutes he settled to the work. Then the Mongol removed the hobbles from the hind legs, and later left the pony entirely free. He walked beside the animal for a long time, and did not attempt to drive him from the cart for at least an hour.

Although Mongols seem unnecessarily rough and almost brutal, I do not believe that any people in the world can handle horses more expertly. From earliest childhood their real home is the back of a pony. Every year, in the spring, a children's race is held at Urga. Boys and girls from four to six years old are tied on horses and ride at full speed over a mile-long course. If a child falls off it receives but scant sympathy and is strapped on again more tightly than before. A Mongol has no respect whatever for a man or woman who cannot ride, and nothing will win his regard as rapidly as expert horsemanship. Strangely enough the Mongols seldom show affection for their ponies, nor do they caress them in any way; consequently, the animals do not enjoy being petted and are prone to kick and bite. My pony, Kublai Khan, was an extraordinary exception to this rule and was as affectionate and gentle as a kitten—but there are few animals like Kublai Khan in Mongolia!

The ponies are small, of course, but they are strong

almost beyond belief, and can stand punishment that would kill an ordinary horse. The Mongols seldom ride except at a trot or a full gallop, and forty to fifty miles a day is not an unusual journey. Moreover, the animals are not fed grain; they must forage on the plains the year round. During the winter, when the grass is dry and sparse, they have poor feeding, but nevertheless are able to withstand the extreme cold. They grow a coat of hair five or six inches in length, and when Kublai Khan arrived in Peking after his long journey across the plains he looked more like a grizzly bear than a horse. He had changed so completely from the sleek, fine-limbed animal we had known in Mongolia that my wife was almost certain he could not be the same pony. He had to be taught to eat carrots, apples, and other vegetables and would only sniff suspiciously at sugar. But in a very short time he learned all the tastes of his city-bred companions.

Horses are cheap in Mongolia, but not extraordinarily so. In the spring a fair pony can be purchased for from thirty to sixty dollars (silver), and especially good ones bring as much as one hundred and fifty dollars. In the fall when the Mongols are confronted with a hard winter, which naturally exacts a certain toll from any herd, ponies sell for about two-thirds of their spring price.

In Urga we had been led to believe that the entire trip to Sain Noin Khan's village could be done in eight days and that game was plentiful along the trail. We had already been on the road five days, making an average of twenty-five miles at each stage, and the natives assured us that it would require at least ten more days of steady travel before we could possibly arrive at our destination; if difficulties arose it might take even longer. Moreover, we had seen only one hare and one marmot, and our traps had yielded virtually nothing. It was perfectly evident that the entire valley had been denuded of animal life by the Mongols, and there was little prospect that conditions would change as long as we remained on such rich grazing grounds.

It was hard to turn back and count the time lost, but it was certainly the wisest course for we knew that there was good collecting on the plains south of Urga, although the fauna would not be as varied as at the place we had hoped to reach. The summer in Mongolia is so short that every day must be made to count if results which are worth the money invested are to be obtained.

Yvette and I were both very despondent that evening when we decided it was necessary to turn back. It was one of those nights when I wished with all my heart that we could sit in front of our own camp fire without the thought of having to "make good" to any one but ourselves. However, once the decision was made, we tried to forget the past days and determined to make up for lost time in the future.

CHAPTER VIII

THE LURE OF THE PLAINS

On Monday, June 16, we left Urga to go south along
the old caravan trail toward Kalgan. Only a few weeks
earlier we had skimmed over the rolling surface in
motor cars, crossing in one day then as many miles of
plains as our own carts could do in ten. But it had another meaning to us now, and the first night as we sat
at dinner in front of the tent and watched the after-
glow fade from the sky behind the pine-crowned ridge
of the Bogdo-ol, we thanked God that for five long
months we could leave the twentieth century with its
roar and rush, and live as the Mongols live; we knew
that the days of discouragement had ended and that we
could learn the secrets of the desert life which are yielded
up to but a chosen few.

Within twenty-five miles of Urga we had seen a
dozen marmots and a species of gopher (*Citellus*) that
was new to us. The next afternoon at two o'clock we
climbed the last long slope from out the Tola River
drainage basin, and reached the plateau which stretches
in rolling waves of plain and desert to the frontier of
China six hundred miles away. Before us three pools
of water flashed like silver mirrors in the sunlight, and
beyond them, tucked away in a sheltered corner of the

hills, stood a little temple surrounded by a cluster of gray-white *yurts*.

Our Mongol learned that the next water was on the far side of a plain thirty-five miles in width, so we camped beside the largest pond. It was a beautiful spot with gently rolling hills on either side, and in front, a level plain cut by the trail's white line.

As soon as the tents were up Yvette and I rode off, accompanied by the lama, carrying a bag of traps. Within three hundred yards of camp we found the first marmot. When it had disappeared underground we carefully buried a steel trap at the entrance of the hole and anchored it securely to an iron tent peg. With rocks and earth we plugged all the other openings, for there are usually five or six tunnels to every burrow. While the work was going on other marmots were watching us curiously from half a dozen mounds, and we set nine traps before it was time to return for dinner.

The two Chinese taxidermists had taken a hundred wooden traps for smaller mammals, and before dark we inspected the places they had found. Already one of them held a gray meadow vole (*Microtus*), quite a different species from those which had been caught along the Tola River, and Yvette discovered one of the larger traps dragged halfway into a hole with a baby marmot safely caught. He was only ten inches long and covered with soft yellow-white fur.

Shortly after daylight the next morning the lama came to our tent to announce that there was a marmot in one of the traps. The boy was as excited as a child

of ten and had been up at dawn. When we were dressed
we followed the Mongol to the first burrow where a fine
marmot was securely caught by the hind leg. A few
yards away we had another female, and the third trap
was pulled far into the hole. A huge male was at the
other end, but he had twisted his body halfway around
a curve in the tunnel and by pulling with all our strength
the Mongol and I could not move him a single inch.
Finally we gave up and had to dig him out. He had
given a wonderful exhibition of strength for so small an
animal.

It was especially gratifying to catch these marmots so
easily, for we had been told in Urga that the Mongols
could not trap them. I was at a loss to understand
why, for they are closely related to the "woodchucks"
of America with which every country boy is familiar.
Later I learned the reason for the failure of the natives.
In the Urga market we saw some double-spring traps
exactly like those of ours, but when I came to examine
them I found they had been made in Russia, and the
springs were so weak that they were almost useless.
These were the only steel traps which the Mongols had
ever seen.

The marmots (*Marmota robusta*) were supposed to
be responsible for the spread of the pneumonia plague
which swept into northern China from Manchuria a few
years ago; but I understand from physicians of the
Rockefeller Foundation in Peking, who especially
investigated the disease, that the animal's connection
with it is by no means satisfactorily determined.

The marmots hibernate during the winter, and retire
to their burrows early in October, not to emerge until
April. When they first come out in the spring their fur
is bright yellow, and the animals contrast beautifully
with the green grass. After the middle of June the
yellow fur begins to slip off in patches, leaving exposed
the new coat, which is exceedingly short and is mouse-
gray in color. Then, of course, the skins are useless for
commercial purposes. As the summer progresses the
fur grows until by September first it has formed a long,
soft coat of rich gray-brown which is of considerable
economic value. The skins are shipped to Europe and
America and during the past winter (1919-1920) were
especially popular as linings for winter coats.

We had an opportunity to see how quickly the de-
mand in the great cities reaches directly to the center of
production thousands of miles away. When we went to
Urga in May prime marmot skins were worth thirty
cents each to the Mongols. Early in October, when we
returned, the hunters were selling the same skins for
one dollar and twenty-five cents apiece.

The natives always shoot the animals. When a Mongol has driven one into its burrow, he lies quietly beside
the hole waiting for the marmot to appear. It may be
twenty minutes or even an hour, but the Oriental pa-
tience takes little note of time. Finally a yellow head
emerges and a pair of shining eyes glance quickly about
in every direction. Of course, they see the Mongol but
he looks only like a mound of earth, and the marmot
raises itself a few inches higher. The hunter lies as

motionless as a log of wood until the animal is well out of its burrow—then he shoots.

The Mongols take advantage of the marmot's curiosity in an amusing and even more effective way. With a dogskin tied to his saddle the native rides over the plain until he reaches a marmot colony. He hobbles his pony at a distance of three or four hundred yards, gets down on his hands and knees, and throws the dogskin over his shoulders. He crawls slowly toward the nearest animal, now and then stopping to bark and shake his head. In an instant, the marmot is all attention. He jumps up and down whistling and barking, but never venturing far from the opening of his burrow.

As the pseudo-dog advances there seems imminent danger that the fat little body will explode from curiosity and excitement. But suddenly the "dog" collapses in the strangest way and the marmot raises on the very tips of his toes to see what it is all about. Then there is a roar, a flash of fire and another skin is added to the millions which have already been sent to the seacoast from outer Mongolia.

Mr. Mamen often spoke of an extraordinary dance which he had seen the marmots perform, and when Mr. and Mrs. MacCallie returned to Kalgan they saw it also. We were never fortunate enough to witness it. Mac said that two marmots stood erect on their hind legs, grasping each other with their front paws, and danced slowly about exactly as though they were waltzing. He agreed with Mamen that it was the most extraordinary and amusing thing he had ever seen an animal do. I can well believe it, for the marmots have many curious habits which would repay close study. The dance could hardly be a mating performance since Mac saw it in late May and by that time the young had already been born.

One morning at the "Marmot Camp," as we named the one where we first began real collecting, Yvette saw six or seven young animals on top of a mound in the green grass. We went there later with a gun and found the little fellows playing like kittens, chasing each other about and rolling over and over. It was hard to make myself bring tragedy into their lives, but we needed them for specimens. A group showing an entire marmot family would be interesting for the Museum; especially so in view of their reported connection with the pneumonic plague. We collected a dozen others before the summer was over to show the complete transition from the first yellow coat to the gray-brown of winter.

Like most rodents, the marmots grow rapidly and have so many young in every litter that they will not soon be exterminated in Mongolia unless the native hunters obtain American steel traps. Even then it would take some years to make a really alarming impression upon the millions which spread over all the plains of northern Mongolia and Manchuria.

Since these marmots are a distinctly northern animal they are a great help in determining the life zones of this part of Asia. We found that their southern limit is at Turin, one hundred and seventy-five miles from Urga. A few scattered families live there, but the real marmot country begins about twenty-five miles farther north.

The first hunting camp was eighty miles south of Urga, after we had passed a succession of low hills and reached what, in prehistoric times, was probably a great lake basin. When our tents were pitched beside the well they seemed pitifully small in the vastness of the plain. The land rolled in placid waves to the far horizon on every hand. It was like a calm sea which is disturbed only by the lazy progress of the ocean swell. Two *yurts,* like the sails of hull-down ships, showed black against the sky-rim where it met the earth. The plain itself seemed at first as flat as a table, for the swells merged indistinguishably into a level whole. It was only when approaching horsemen dipped for a little out of sight and the depressions swallowed them up that we realized the unevenness of the land.

Camp was hardly made before our Mongol neighbors began to pay their formal calls. A picturesque fellow, blazing with color, would dash up to our tent at a full gallop, slide off and hobble his pony almost in a single motion. With a *"sai bina"* of greeting he would squat in the door, produce his bottle of snuff and offer us a pinch. There was a quiet dignity about these plains dwellers which was wonderfully appealing. They were seldom unduly curious, and when we indicated that the visit was at an end, they left at once.

Sometimes they brought bowls of curded milk, or great lumps of cheese as presents, and in return we gave cigarettes or now and then a cake of soap. Having been told in Urga that soap was especially appreciated by the Mongols, I had brought a supply of red, blue, and green cakes which had a scent even more wonderful than the color. I can't imagine why they like it, for it is carefully put away and never used.

Strangely enough, the Mongols have no word for "thank you" other than "*sai*" (good), but when they wish to express approbation, and usually when saying "good-by," they put up the thumb with the fingers closed. In Yün-nan and eastern Tibet we noted the same custom among the aboriginal tribesmen. I wonder if it is merely a coincidence that in the gladiatorial contests of ancient Rome "thumbs up" meant mercy or approval!

The Mongols told us that in the rolling ground to the east of camp we could surely find antelope. The first morning my wife and I went out alone. We trotted steadily for an hour, making for the summit of a rise seven or eight miles from camp. Yvette held the ponies, while I sat down to sweep the country with my glasses. Directly in front of us two small valleys converged into a larger one, and almost immediately I discovered half a dozen orange-yellow forms in its very bottom about two miles away. They were antelope quietly feeding. In a few moments I made out two more close together, and then four off at the right. After my wife had found them with her glasses we sat down to plan the stalk.

It was obvious that we should try to cross the two small depressions which debouched into the main valley and approach from behind the hill crest nearest to the gazelles. We trotted slowly across the gully while the antelope were in sight, and then swung around at full gallop under the protection of the rising ground. We came up just opposite to the herd and dismounted, but were fully six hundred yards away. Suddenly one of those impulses which the hunter never can explain sent them off like streaks of yellow light, but they turned on the opposite hillside, slowed down, and moved uncertainly up the valley.

Much to our surprise four of the animals detached themselves from the others and crossed the depression in our direction. When we saw that they were really coming we threw ourselves into the saddles and galloped forward to cut them off. Instantly the antelope increased their speed and literally flew up the hill slope. I shouted to Yvette to watch the holes and shook the reins over Kublai Khan's neck. Like a bullet he was off. I could feel his great muscles flowing between my knees but otherwise there seemed hardly a motion of his body in the long, smooth run. Standing straight up in the stirrups, I glanced back at my wife who was sitting her chestnut stallion as lightly as a butterfly. Hat gone, hair streaming, the thrill of it all showed in every line of her body. She was running a close second, almost at my side. I saw a marmot hole flash by. A second death trap showed ahead and I swung Kublai Khan to the right. Another and another followed, but the pony leaped them like a cat. The beat of the fresh, clean air; the rush of the splendid horse; the sight of the yellow forms fleeing like wind-blown ribbons across our path—

all this set me mad with excitement and a wild exhilaration. Suddenly I realized that I was yelling like an Indian. Yvette, too, was screaming in sheer delight.

The antelope were two hundred yards away when I tightened on the reins. Kublai Khan stiffened and stopped in twenty yards. The first shot was low and to the left, but it gave the range. At the second, the rearmost animal stumbled, recovered itself, and ran wildly about in a circle. I missed him twice, and he disappeared over a little hill. Leaping into the saddle, we tore after the wounded animal. As we thundered over the rise I heard my wife screaming frantically and saw her pointing to the right where the antelope was lying down. There was just one more shell in the gun and my pockets were empty. I fired again at fifty yards and the gazelle rolled over, dead.

Leading our horses, Yvette and I walked up to the beautiful orange-yellow form lying in the fresh, green grass. We both saw its horns in the same instant and hugged each other in sheer delight. At this time of the year the bucks are seldom with the does and then only in the largest herds. This one was in full pelage, spotless and with the hair unworn. Moreover, it had finer horns than any other which we killed during the entire trip.

Kublai Khan looked at the dead animal and arched his neck, as much as to say, "Yes, I ran him down. He had to quit when I really got started." My wife held the pony's head, while I hoisted the antelope to his back and strapped it behind the saddle. He watched the proceedings interestedly but without a tremor, and even when I mounted, he paid not the slightest attention to the head dangling on his flanks. Thereby he showed that he was a very exceptional pony. In the weeks which followed he proved it a hundred times, and I came to love him as I have never loved another animal.

Yvette and I trotted slowly back to camp, thrilled with the excitement of the wild ride. We began to realize that we were lucky to have escaped without broken necks. The race taught us never again to attempt to guide our ponies away from the marmot holes which spotted the plains, for the horses could see them better than we could and all their lives had known that they meant death.

That morning was our initiation into what is the finest sport we have ever known. Hunting from a motor car is undeniably exciting at first, but a real sportsman can never care for it very long. The antelope does not have a chance against gas and steel and a long-range rifle. On horseback the conditions are reversed. An antelope can run twice as fast as the best horse living. It can see as far as a man with prism binoculars. All the odds are in the animal's favor except two—its fatal desire to run in a circle about the pursuer, and the use of a high-power rifle. But even then an antelope three hundred yards away, going at a speed of fifty miles an hour, is not an easy target.

Of course, the majority of sportsmen will say that it cannot be done with any certainty—until they go to Mongolia and do it themselves! But, as I remarked in

a previous chapter, conditions on the plains are so unusual that shooting in other parts of the world is no cri-
terion. After one gets the range of an animal which,
like the antelope, has a smooth, even run, it is not so
difficult to hit as one might imagine. Practice is the
great essential. At the beginning I averaged one antelope to every eight cartridges, but later my score was
one to three.

We spent the afternoon at the new camp, setting
traps and preparing for the days to come—days in
which we knew, from long experience, we would have
every waking moment full of work. The nights were
shortening rapidly, and the sun did not dip below the
rim of our vast, flat world until half past seven. Then
there was an hour of delightful, lingering twilight, when
the stars began to show in tiny points of light; by nine
o'clock the brooding silence of the Mongolian night had
settled over all the plain.

Daylight came at four o'clock, and before the sun
rose we had finished breakfast. Our traps held five
marmots and a beautiful golden-yellow polecat (*Mus-
tela*). I have never seen such an incarnation of fury as
this animal presented. It might have been the original
of the Chinese dragon, except for its small size. Its
long, slender body twisted and turned with incredible
swiftness, every hair was bristling, and its snarling little
face emitted horrible squeaks and spitting squeals. It
seemed to be cursing us in every language of the polecat tribe.

The fierce little beast was evidently bent upon a night

raid on a marmot family. We could imagine easily into what terror the tiny demon would throw a nest of marmots comfortably snuggled together in the bottom of their burrow. Probably it would be most interested in the babies, and undoubtedly would destroy every one within a few moments. All the weasel family, to which the polecat belongs, kill for the pure joy of killing, and in China one such animal will entirely depopulate a hen-roost in a single night.

At six o'clock Yvette and I left camp with the lama and rode northeast. The plain swept away in long, grassy billows, and at every rise I stopped for a moment to scan the horizon with my glasses. Within half an hour we discovered a herd of antelope six or seven hundred yards away. They saw us instantly and trotted nervously about, staring in our direction.

Dropping behind the crest of the rise, I directed the lama to ride toward them from behind while we swung about to cut them off. He was hardly out of sight when we heard a snort and a rush of pounding hoofs. With a shout to Yvette I loosened the reins over Kublai Khan's neck, and he shot forward like a yellow arrow. Yvette was close beside me, leaning far over her pony's neck. We headed diagonally toward the herd, and they gradually swung toward us as though drawn by a powerful magnet. On we went, down into a hollow and up again on its slope. We could not spare the horses for the antelope were already over the crest and lost to view, but our horses took the hill at full speed, and from the summit we could see the herd fairly on our course, three hundred yards away.

Kublai Khan braced himself like a polo pony when he felt the pressure of my knees, and I opened fire almost under his nose. At the crack of the rifle there was a spurt of brown dust near the leading animal. "High and to the left," shouted Yvette, and I held a little lower for the second trial. The antelope dropped like a piece of white paper, shot through the neck. I paced the distance and found it to be three hundred and sixty-seven yards. It seemed a very long shot then, but later I found that almost none of my antelope were killed at less than three hundred yards.

As I came up to Kublai Khan with the dead animal, I accidentally struck him on the flank with my rifle in such a way that he was badly frightened. He galloped off, and Yvette had a hard chase before he finally allowed her to catch him. Had I been alone I should probably have had a long walk to camp.

It taught us never to hunt without a companion, if it could possibly be avoided. If your horse runs away, you may be left many miles from water, with rather serious consequences. I think there is nothing which makes me feel more helpless than to be alone on the plains without a horse. For miles and miles there is only the rolling grassland or the wide sweep of desert, with never a house or tree to break the low horizon. It seems so futile to walk, your own legs carry you so slowly and such a pitifully short distance, in these vast spaces.

To be left alone in a small boat on the open sea is

exactly similar. You feel so very, very small and you realize then what an insignificant part of nature you really are. I have felt it, too, amid vast mountains when I have been toiling up a peak which stretched thousands of feet above me with others rearing their majestic forms on every side. Then, nature seems almost alive and full of menace; something to be fought and conquered by brain and will.

Early in our work upon the plains we learned how easy it is to lose one's way. The vast sea of land seems absolutely flat, but in reality it is a gently rolling surface full of slopes and hollows, every one of which looks exactly like the others. But after a time we developed a *land sense*. The Mongols all have it to an extraordinary degree. We could drop an antelope on the plain and leave it for an hour or more. With a quick glance about our lama would fix the place in his mind, and dash off on a chase which might carry us back and forth toward every point of the compass. When it was time to return, he would head his pony unerringly for that single spot on the plain and take us back as straight as the flight of an arrow.

At first it gave him unceasing enjoyment when we became completely lost, but in a very short time we learned to note the position of the sun, the character of the ground, and the direction of the wind. Then we began to have more confidence in ourselves. But only by years of training can one hope even to approximate the Mongols. They have been born and reared upon the plains, and have the inheritance of unknown generations whose very life depended upon their ability to come and go at will. To them, the hills, the sun, the grass, the sand—all have become the street signs of the desert.

In the afternoon of our second day I remained at the tents to measure specimens, while Yvette and the lama rode out toward the scene of our morning hunt to locate an antelope which one of our Mongol neighbors had reported dead not far away. At six o'clock they came galloping back with the news that there were two gazelles within three miles of camp. I saddled Kublai Khan and left with them at once. Twenty minutes of steady trotting brought us to the summit of a slope, where we could see the animals quietly feeding not five hundred yards away.

It was just possible to stalk them for a long-range shot, and slipping off my pony, I flattened out upon the ground. On hands and knees, and sometimes at full length, I wormed my way through the grass for one hundred yards. The cover ended there and I must shoot or come into full view of the gazelles. They were so far away that the front sight entirely covered the animals, and to increase the difficulty, both were walking slowly. The first bullet struck low and to the right, but the antelope only jumped and stared fixedly in my direction; at the second shot one went down. The other animal dashed away like a flash of lightning, and although I sent a bullet after its white rump-patch, the shot was hopeless.

The antelope I had knocked over got to its feet and tried desperately to get away, but the lama leaped on his pony and caught it by one hind leg. My automatic pistol was not in working order, and it was necessary to knife the poor beast—a job which I hate like poison. The lama walked away a dozen yards and covered his face with the sleeve of his gown. It is against the laws of the Buddhist religion to take the life of any animal or even to see it done, although there are no restrictions as to eating flesh.

With a blanket the Mongol made a seat for himself on his pony's haunches, and threw the antelope across his saddle; then we trotted back to camp into the painted western sky, with the cool night air bringing to us the scent of newborn grass. We would not have exchanged our lot that night with any one on earth.

CHAPTER IX

HUNTING ON THE TURIN PLAIN

After ten days we left the "Antelope Camp" to visit the Turin plain where we had seen much game on the way to Urga. One by one our Mongol neighbors rode up to say "farewell," and each to present us with a silk scarf as a token of friendship and good will. We received an invitation to stop for tea at the *yurt* of an old man who had manifested an especial interest in us, but it was a very dirty *yurt,* and the preparations for tea were so uninviting that we managed to exit gracefully before it was finally served.

Yvette photographed the entire family including half a dozen dogs, a calf, and two babies, much to their enjoyment. When we rode off, our hands were heaped with cheese and slabs of mutton which were discarded as soon as we had dropped behind a slope. Mongol hospitality is whole-souled and generously given, but one must be very hungry to enjoy their food.

A day and a half of traveling was uneventful, for herds of sheep and horses indicated the presence of *yurts* among the hills. Game will seldom remain where there are Mongols. Although it was the first of July, we found a heavy coating of ice on the lower sides of a deep well. The water was about fifteen feet below the level

A LONE CAMP ON THE DESERT

of the plain, and the ice would probably remain all summer. Moreover, it is said that the wells never freeze even during the coldest winter.

The changes of temperature were more rapid than in any other country in which I have ever hunted. It was hot during the day—about 85° Fahrenheit—but the instant the sun disappeared we needed coats, and our fur sleeping bags were always acceptable at night.

We were one hundred and fifty miles from Urga and were still going slowly south, when we had our next real hunting camp. Great bands of antelope were working northward from the Gobi Desert to the better grazing on the grass-covered Turin plain. We encountered the main herd one evening about six o'clock, and it was a sight which made us gasp for breath. We were shifting camp, and my wife and I were trotting along parallel to the carts which moved slowly over the trail a mile away. We had had a delightful, as well as a profitable, day. Yvette had been busy with her camera, while I picked up an antelope, a bustard, three hares, and half a dozen marmots. We were loafing in our saddles, when suddenly we caught sight of the cook standing on his cart frantically signaling us to come.

In ten seconds our ponies were flying toward the caravan, while we mentally reviewed every accident which possibly could have happened to the boys. Lü met us twenty yards from the trail, trembling with excitement and totally incoherent. He could only point to the south and stammer, "Too many antelope. Over there. Too many, too many."

I slipped off Kublai Khan's back and put up the glasses. Certainly there were animals, but I thought they must be sheep or ponies. Hundreds were in sight, feeding in one vast herd and in many smaller groups. Then I remembered that the nearest well was twenty miles away; therefore they could not be horses. I looked again and knew they must be antelope—not in hundreds, but in thousands.

Mr. Larsen in Urga had told us of herds like this, but we had never hoped to see one. Yet there before us, as far as the eye could reach, was a yellow mass of moving forms. In a moment Yvette and I had left the carts. There was no possibility of concealment, and our only chance was to run the herd. When we were perhaps half a mile away the nearest animals threw up their heads and began to stamp and run about, only to stop again and stare at us. We kept on very slowly, edging nearer every moment. Suddenly they decided that we were really dangerous, and the herd strung out like a regiment of yellow-coated soldiers.

Kublai Khan had seen the antelope almost as soon as we left the carts, and although he had already traveled forty miles that day, was nervously champing the bit with head up and ears erect. When at last I gave him the word, he gathered himself for one terrific spring; down went his head and he dashed forward with every ounce of strength behind his flying legs. His run was the long, smooth stride of a thoroughbred, and it sent the blood surging through my veins in a wild thrill of exhilaration. Once only I glanced back at Yvette. She

was almost at my side. Her hair had loosened and was
flying back like a veil behind her head. Tense with excitement, eyes shining, she was heedless of everything
save those skimming yellow forms before us. It was
useless to look for holes; ere I had seen one we were over
or around it. With head low down and muzzle out, my
pony needed not the slightest touch to guide him. He
knew where we were going and the part he had to
play.

More than a thousand antelope were running diagonally across our course. It was a sight to stir the gods;
a thing to give one's life to see. But when we were
almost near enough to shoot, the herd suddenly swerved
heading directly away from us. In an instant we were
enveloped in a whirling cloud of dust through which the
flying animals were dimly visible like phantom figures.
Kublai Khan was choked, and his hot breath rasped
sharply through his nostrils, but he plunged on and on
into that yellow cloud. Standing in my stirrups, I fired
six times at the wraithlike forms ahead as fast as I could
work the lever of my rifle. Of course, it was useless, but
just the same I had to shoot.

In about a mile the great herd slowed down and
stopped. We could see hundreds of animals on every
side, in groups of fifty or one hundred. Probably two
thousand antelope were in sight at once and many more
were beyond the sky rim to the west. We gave the
ponies ten minutes' rest, and had another run as unsuccessful as the first. Then a third and fourth. The antelope, for some strange reason, would not cross our path,

but always turned straight away before we were near enough to shoot.

After an hour we returned to the carts—for Yvette was exhausted from excitement—and the lama took her place. We left the great herd and turned southward, parallel to the road. A mile away we found more antelope; at least a thousand were scattered about feeding quietly like those we had driven north. It seemed as though all the gazelles in Mongolia had concentrated on those few miles of plain.

The ponies were so exhausted that we decided to try a drive and leave the main herd in peace. When we were concealed from view in the bottom of a land swell I slipped off and hobbled Kublai Khan. The poor fellow was so tired he could only stand with drooping head, even though there was rich grass beneath his feet. I sent the lama in a long circle to get behind the herd, while I crawled a few hundred yards away and snuggled out of sight into an old wolf den.

I watched the antelope for fifteen minutes through my binoculars. They were feeding in a vast semicircle, entirely unconscious of my presence. Suddenly every head went up; they stared fixedly toward the west for a moment, and were off like the wind. About five hundred drew together in a compact mass, but a dozen smaller herds scattered wildly, running in every direction except toward me. They had seen the lama before he had succeeded in completely encircling them, and the drive was ruined.

The Mongols kill great numbers of antelope in just

this way. When a herd has been located, a line of men will conceal themselves at distances of two or three hundred yards, while as many more get behind the animals and drive them toward the waiting hunters. Sometimes the gazelles almost step on the natives and become so frightened that they run the gantlet of the entire firing line.

I did not have the heart to race again with our exhausted ponies, and we turned back toward the carts which were out of sight. Scores of antelope, singly or in pairs, were visible on the sky line and as we rode to the summit of a little rise a herd of fifty appeared almost below us. We paid no attention to them; but suddenly my pony stopped with ears erect. He looked back at me, as much as to say, "Don't you see those antelope?" and began gently pulling at the reins. I could feel him tremble with eagerness and excitement. "Well, old chap," I said, "if you are as keen as all that, let's give them a run."

With a magnificent burst of speed Kublai Khan launched himself toward the fleeing animals. They circled beautifully, straight into the eye of the sun, which lay like a great red ball upon the surface of the plain. We were still three hundred yards away and gaining rapidly, but I had to shoot; in a moment I would be blinded by the sun. As the flame leaped from my rifle, we heard the dull thud of a bullet on flesh; at the second shot, another; and then a third. *"Sanga"* (three), yelled the lama, and dashed forward, wild with excitement.

The three gazelles lay almost the same distance apart, each one shot through the body. It was interesting evidence that the actions of working the lever on my rifle and aiming, and the speed of the antelope, varied only by a fraction of a second. In this case, brain and eye and hand had functioned perfectly. Needless to say, I do not always shoot like that.

Two of the antelope were yearling bucks, and one was a large doe. The lama took the female on his pony, and I strapped the other two on Kublai Khan. When I mounted, he was carrying a weight of two hundred and eighty-five pounds, yet he kept his steady "homeward trot" without a break until we reached the carts six miles away.

Yvette had been afraid that we would miss the well in the gathering darkness, and had made a "dry camp" beside the road. We had only a little water for ourselves; but my pony's nose was full of dust, and I knew how parched his throat must be, so I divided my supply with him. The poor animal was so frightened by the dish, that he would only snort and back away; even when I wet his nose with some of the precious fluid, he would not drink.

The success of our work upon the plains depended largely upon Kublai Khan. He was only a Mongol pony but he was just as great, in his own way, as was the Tartar emperor whose name he bore. Whatever it was I asked him to do, he gave his very best. Can you wonder that I loved him?

Within a fortnight from the time I bought him, he

became a perfect hunting pony. The secret of it all was that he liked the game as well as I. Traveling with the carts bored him exceedingly but the instant game appeared he was all excitement. Often he saw antelope before we did. We might be trotting slowly over the plains, when suddenly he would jerk his head erect and begin to pull gently at the reins; when I reached down to take my rifle from the holster, he would tremble with eagerness to be off.

In hunting antelope you should ride slowly toward the animals, drawing nearer gradually. They are so accustomed to see Mongols that they will not begin to run in earnest until a man is five or six hundred yards away, but when they are really off, a fast pony is the great essential. The time to stop is just before the animals cross your path, and then you must stop quickly. Kublai Khan learned the trick immediately. As soon as he felt the pressure of my knees, and the slightest pull upon the reins, his whole body stiffened and he braced himself like a polo pony. It made not the slightest difference to him whether I shot from his back or directly under his nose; he stood quietly watching the running antelope. When we were riding across the plains if a bird ran along the ground or a hare jumped out of the grass, he was after it like a dog. Often I would find myself flying toward an animal which I had never seen.

Yvette's pony was useless for hunting antelope. Instead of heading diagonally toward the gazelles he would always attempt to follow the herd. When it was time to stop I would have to put all my strength upon the reins and the horse would come into a slow gallop and then a trot.   Seconds of valuable time would be wasted before I could begin to shoot.   I tried half a dozen other ponies, but they were all as bad.   They did not have the intelligence or the love of hunting which made Kublai Khan so valuable.

The morning after encountering the great herd, we camped at a well thirty miles north of the Turin monastery.   Three or four *yurts* were scattered about, and a caravan of two hundred and fifty camels was resting in a little hollow.   From the door of our tent we could see the blue summit of the Turin "mountain," and have in the foreground a perpetual moving picture of camels, horses, sheep, goats, and cattle seeking water. All day long hundreds of animals crowded about the well, while one or two Mongols filled the troughs by means of wooden buckets.

The life about the wells is always interesting, for they are points of concentration for all wanderers on the plains.   Just as we pitch our tents and make ourselves at home, so great caravans arrive with tired, laden camels.   The huge brutes kneel, while their packs are being removed, and then stand in a long line, patiently waiting until their turn comes to drink.   Groups of ten or twelve crowd about the trough; then, majestically swinging their padded feet, they move slowly to one side, kneel upon the ground, and sleepily chew their cuds until all the herd has joined them.   Sometimes the caravans wait for several days to rest their animals and

let them feed; sometimes they vanish in the first gray
light of dawn.

On the Turin plain we had a delightful glimpse of
antelope babyhood. The great herds which we had
found were largely composed of does just ready to drop
their young, and after a few days they scattered widely
into groups of from five to twenty.

We found the first baby antelope on June 27.
We had seen half a dozen females circling restlessly
about, and suspected that their fawns could not be far
away. Sure enough, our Mongol discovered one of the
little fellows in the flattest part of the flat plain. It
was lying motionless with its neck stretched out, just
where its mother had told it to remain when she saw us
riding toward her.

Yvette called to me, "Oh, please, please catch it. We
can raise it on milk and it will make such an adorable
pet."

"Oh, yes," I said, "let's do. I'll get it for you. You
can put it in your hat till we go back to camp."

In blissful ignorance I dismounted and slowly went
toward the little animal. There was not the slightest
motion until I tossed my outspread shooting coat.
Then I saw a flash of brown, a bobbing white rump-
patch, and a tiny thing, no larger than a rabbit, speed-
ing over the plain. The baby was somewhat "wab-
bly," to be sure, for this was probably the first time
it had ever tried its slender legs, but after a few hundred yards it ran as steadily as its mother.

I was so surprised that for a moment I simply stared.

Then I leaped into the saddle and Kublai Khan rushed after the diminutive brown fawn. It was a good half mile before we had the little chap under the pony's nose but the race was by no means ended. Mewing with fright, it swerved sharply to the left and ere we could swing about, it had gained a hundred yards. Again and again we were almost on it, but every time it dodged and got away. After half an hour my pony was gasping for breath, and I changed to Yvette's chestnut stallion. The Mongol joined me and we had another run, but we might have been pursuing a streak of shifting sunlight. Finally we had to give it up and watch the tiny thing bob away toward its mother, who was circling about in the distance.

There were half a dozen other fawns upon the plain, but they all treated us alike and my wife's hat was empty when we returned to camp. These antelope probably had been born not more than two or three days before we found them. Later, after a chase of more than a mile, we caught one which was only a few hours old. Had it not injured itself when dodging between my pony's legs we could never have secured it at all.

Thus, nature, in the great scheme of life, has provided for her antelope children by blessing them with undreamed-of speed and only during the first days of babyhood could a wolf catch them on the open plain. When they are from two to three weeks old they run with the females in herds of six or eight, and you cannot imagine what a pretty sight it is to see the little fellows skimming like tiny, brown chickens beside their mothers. There is another wonderful provision for their life upon the desert. The digestive fluids of the stomach act upon the starch in the vegetation which they eat so that it forms sufficient water for their needs. Therefore, some species never drink.

The antelope choose a flat plain on which to give birth to their young in order to be well away from the wolves which are their greatest enemy; and the fawns are taught to lie absolutely motionless upon the ground until they know that they have been discovered. Apparently they are all born during the last days of June and in the first week of July. The great herds which we encountered were probably moving northward both to obtain better grazing and to drop their young on the Turin plain. During this period the old bucks go off singly into the rolling ground, and the herds are composed only of does and yearling males. It was always possible to tell at once if an antelope had a fawn upon the plain, for she would run in a wide circle around the spot and refuse to be driven away.

We encountered only two species of antelope between Kalgan and Urga. The one of which I have been writing, and with which we became best acquainted, was the Mongolian gazelle (*Gazella gutturosa*). The other was the goitered gazelle (*Gazella subgutturosa*). In the western Gobi, the Prjevalski gazelle (*Gazella prjevalski*) is more abundant than the other species, but it never reaches the region which we visited.

The goitered antelope is seldom found on the rolling

meadowlands between Kalgan and Panj-kiang on the south, or between Turin and Urga on the north, according to our observations; they keep almost entirely to the Gobi Desert between Panj-kiang and Turin, and we often saw them among the "nigger heads" or tussocks in the most arid parts. The Mongolian gazelle, on the other hand, is most abundant in the grasslands both north and south of the Gobi, but nevertheless has a continuous distribution across the plateau between Kalgan and Urga.

On our northward trip in May, when we took motion pictures of the antelope on the Panj-kiang plain, both species were present, but the goitered gazelle far outnumbered the others—which is unusual in that locality. It could always be distinguished from the Mongolian gazelle because of its smaller size, darker coloring, and the long tail which it carries straight up in the air at right angles to the back; the Mongolian antelope has an exceedingly short tail. The horns of both species differ considerably in shape and can easily be distinguished.

During the winter these antelope develop a coat of very long, soft hair which is light brown-gray in color strongly tinged with rufous on the head and face. Its summer pelage is a beautiful orange-fawn. The winter coat is shed during May, and the animals lose their short summer hair in late August and early September.

Both species have a greatly enlarged larynx from which the goitered gazelle derives its name. What purpose this extraordinary character serves the animal, I

am at a loss to know.   Certainly it is not to give them
an exceptional "voice"; for, when wounded, I have
heard them make only a deep-toned roar which was by
no means loud. Specimens of the larynx which we
preserved in formalin are now being prepared for
anatomical study.

Although the two species inhabit the same locality,
they keep well by themselves and only once, on the
Panj-kiang plain, did we see them running together in
the same herd; then it was probably because they were
frightened by the car.   I doubt if they ever interbreed
except in rare instances.

The fact that these animals can develop such an extraordinary speed was a great surprise to me, as undoubtedly it will be to most naturalists. Had we not
been able to determine it accurately by means of the
speedometers on our cars, I should never have dared
state that they could reach fifty-five or sixty miles an
hour.   It must be remembered that the animals can
continue at such a high speed only for a short distance
—perhaps half a mile—and will never exert themselves
to the utmost unless they are thoroughly frightened.
They would run just fast enough to keep well away
from the cars or our horses, and it was only when we
began to shoot that they showed what they were capable
of doing. When the bullets began to scatter about them
they would seem to flatten several inches and run at
such a terrific speed that their legs appeared only as a
blur.

Of course, they have developed their fleetness as a

protection from enemies. Their greatest menace is the wolves, but since we demonstrated that these animals cannot travel faster than about thirty miles an hour, the antelope are perfectly safe unless they happen to be caught off their guard. To prevent just this, the gazelles usually keep well out on the open plains and avoid rocks or abrupt hills which would furnish cover for a wolf. Of course, they often go into the rolling ground, but it is usually where the slopes are gradual and where they have sufficient space in which to protect themselves.

The gazelles have a perfectly smooth, even run when going at full speed. I have often seen them bound along when not particularly frightened, but never when they are really trying to get away in the shortest possible time. The front limbs, as in the case of a deer, act largely as supports and the real motive power comes from the hind legs. If an antelope has only a front leg broken no living horse can catch it, but with a shattered hind limb my pony could run it down. I have already related (see page 49) how, in a car, we pursued an antelope with both front legs broken below the knee; even then, it reached a speed of fifteen miles an hour. The Mongolian plains are firm and hard with no bushes or other obstructions and, consequently, are especially favorable for rapid travel.

The cheetah, or hunting leopard of Africa, has the reputation of being able to reach a greater speed, for a short dash, than any other animal in that country, and I have often wondered how it would fare in a race

with a Mongolian gazelle. Unfortunately, conditions
in Africa are not favorable for the use of automobiles
in hunting, and no actual facts as to the speed of the
cheetah are available.

At this camp, and during the journey back to Urga,
we had many glorious hunts. Each one held its own
individual fascination, for no two were just alike; and
every day we learned something new about the life history of the Mongolian antelope. We needed specimens for a group in the new Hall of Asiatic Life in the
American Museum of Natural History, as well as a
series representing all ages of both males and females
for scientific study. When we returned to Urga we
had them all.

The hunting of large game was only one aspect of
our work. We usually returned to camp about two
o'clock in the afternoon. As soon as tiffin had been
eaten my wife worked at her photography, while I bus-
ied myself over the almost innumerable details of the
preparation and cataloguing of our specimens. About
six o'clock, accompanied by the two Chinese taxidermists carrying bags of traps, we would leave the
tents. Sometimes we would walk several miles, meanwhile carefully scrutinizing the ground for holes or
traces of mammal workings, and set eighty or one hundred traps. We might find a colony of meadow voles
(*Microtus*) where dozens of "runways" betrayed their
presence, or discover the burrows of the desert hamster
(*Cricetulus*). These little fellows, not larger than a

house mouse, have their tiny feet enveloped in soft fur, like the slippers of an Eskimo baby.

As we walked back to camp in the late afternoon, we often saw a kangaroo rat (*Alactaga mongolica?*) jumping across the plain, and when we had driven it into a hole, we could be sure to catch it in a trap the following morning. They are gentle little creatures, with huge, round eyes, long, delicate ears, and tails tufted at the end like the feathers on an arrow's shaft. The name expresses exactly what they are like—diminutive kangaroos—but, of course, they are rodents and not marsupials. During the glacial period of the early Pleistocene, about one hundred thousand years ago, we know from fossil remains that there were great invasions into Europe of most of these types of tiny mammals, which we were catching during this delightful summer on the Mongolian plains.

After two months we regretfully turned back toward Urga. Our summer was to be divided between the plains on the south and the forests to the north of the sacred city, and the first half of the work had been completed. The results had been very satisfactory, and our boxes contained five hundred specimens; but our hearts were sad. The wide sweep of the limitless, grassy sea, the glorious morning rides, and the magic of the starlit nights had filled our blood. Even the lure of the unknown forests could not make us glad to go, for the plains had claimed us as their own.

CHAPTER X

AN ADVENTURE IN THE LAMA CITY

Late on a July afternoon my wife and I stood disconsolately in the middle of the road on the outskirts of Urga. We had halted because the road had ended abruptly in a muddy river. Moreover, the river was where it had no right to be, for we had traveled that road before and had found only a tiny trickle across its dusty surface. We were disconsolate because we wished to camp that night in Urga, and there were abundant signs that it could not be done.

At least the Mongols thought so, and we had learned that what a Mongol does not do had best "give us pause." They had accepted the river with Oriental philosophy and had made their camps accordingly. Already a score of tents dotted the hillside, and *argul* fires were smoking in the doorways. Hundreds of carts were drawn up in an orderly array while a regiment of oxen wandered about the hillside or sleepily chewed their cuds beside the loads. In a few hours or days or weeks the river would disappear, and then they would go on to Urga. Meanwhile, why worry?

Two adventurous spirits, with a hundred camels, tried to cross. We watched the huge beasts step majestically into the water, only to huddle together in a yel-

133

low-brown mass when they reached midstream. All
their dignity fled, and they became merely frightened
mountains of flesh amid a chaos of writhing necks and
wildly switching tails.

But stranger still was a motor car standing on a
partly submerged island between two branches of the
torrent. We learned later that its owners had successfully navigated the first stream and entered the second. A flooded carburetor had resulted, and ere the
car was again in running order, the water had risen
sufficiently to maroon them on the island.

My wife and I both lack the philosophical nature
of the Oriental, and it was a sore trial to camp within
rifle shot of Urga. But we did not dare leave our
carts, loaded with precious specimens, to the care of
servants and the curiosity of an ever increasing horde
of Mongols.

For a well-nigh rainless month we had been hunting
upon the plains, while only one hundred and fifty miles
away Urga had had an almost daily deluge. In mid-
summer heavy rain-clouds roll southward to burst
against "God's Mountain," which rears its green-clad
summits five thousand feet above the valley. Then it
is only a matter of hours before every streamlet becomes a swollen torrent. But they subside as quickly
as they rise, and the particular river which barred our
road had lost its menace before the sun had risen in a
cloudless morning sky. All the valley seemed in motion. We joined the motley throng of camels, carts,
and horsemen; and even the motor car coughed and

wheezed its way to Urga under the stimulus of two bearded Russians.

We made our camp on a beautiful bit of lawn within a few hundred yards of one of the most interesting of all the Urga temples. It is known to the foreigners in the city as "God's Brother's House," for it was the residence of the Hutukhtu's late brother. The temple presents a bewildering collection of carved gables and gayly painted pavilions flaunting almost every color of the rainbow. Yvette and I were consumed with curiosity to see what was contained within the high palisades which surround the buildings. We knew it would be impossible to obtain permission for her to go inside, and one evening as we were walking along the walls we glanced through the open gate. No one was in sight and from somewhere in the far interior we heard the moaning chant of many voices. Evidently the lamas were at their evening prayers.

We stepped inside the door intending only to take a rapid look. The entire court was deserted, so we slipped through the second gate and stood just at the entrance of the main temple, the "holy of holies." In the half darkness we could see the tiny points of yellow light where candles burned before the altar. On either side was a double row of kneeling lamas, their wailing chant broken by the clash of cymbals and the boom of drums.

Beside the temple were a hideous foreign house and an enormous *yurt*—evidently the former residences of "God's Brother"; in the corners of the compound were ornamental pavilions painted green and red. Except for these, the court was empty.

Suddenly there was a stir among the lamas, and we dashed away like frightened rabbits, dodging behind the gateposts until we were safe outside. It was not until some days later that we learned what a really dangerous thing it was to do, for the temple is one of the holiest in Urga, and in it women are never allowed. Had a Mongol seen us, our camp would have been stormed by a mob of frenzied lamas.

A few days later we had an experience which demonstrates how quickly trouble can arise where religious superstitions are involved. My wife and I had put the motion picture camera in one of the carts and, with our Mongol driving, went to the summit of the hill above the Lama City to film a panoramic view of Urga. We, ourselves, were on horseback. After getting the pictures, we drove down the main street of the city and stopped before the largest temple, which I had photographed several times before.

As soon as the motion picture machine was in position, about five hundred lamas gathered about us. It was a good-natured crowd, however, and we had almost finished work, when a "black Mongol" (i.e., one with a queue, not a lama) pushed his way among the priests and began to harangue them violently. In a few moments he boldly grasped me by the arm. Fearing that trouble might arise, I smiled and said, in Chinese, that we were going away. The Mongol began to gesticulate wildly and attempted to pull me with him farther into the crowd of lamas, who also were becoming excited. I was being separated from Yvette, and realizing that it would be dangerous to get far away from her, I suddenly wrenched my arm free and threw the Mongol to the ground; then I rushed through the line of lamas surrounding Yvette, and we backed up against the cart.

I had an automatic pistol in my pocket, but it would have been suicide to shoot except as a last resort. When a Mongol "starts anything" he is sure to finish it; he is not like a Chinese, who will usually run at the first shot. We stood for at least three minutes with that wall of scowling brutes ten feet away. They were undecided what to do and were only waiting for a leader to close in. One huge beast over six feet tall was just in front of me, and as I stood with my fingers crooked about the trigger of the automatic in my pocket, I thought, "If you start, I'm going to nail you anyway."

Just at this moment of indecision our Mongol leaped on my wife's pony, shouted that he was going to Duke Loobitsan Yangsen, an influential friend of ours, and dashed away. Instantly attention turned from us to him. Fifty men were on horseback in a second, flying after him at full speed. I climbed into the cart, shouting to Yvette to jump on Kublai Khan and run; but she would not leave me. At full speed we dashed down the hill, the plunging horses scattering lamas right and left. Our young Mongol had saved us from a situation which momentarily might have become critical.

At the entrance to the main street of Urga below the Lama City I saw the black Mongol who had started all the trouble. I jumped to the ground, seized him by the collar and one leg, and attempted to throw him into the cart for I had a little matter to settle with him which could best be done to my satisfaction where we were without spectators.

At the same instant a burly policeman, wearing a saber fully five feet long, seized my horse by the bridle. At the black Mongol's instigation (who, I discovered, was himself a policeman) he had been waiting to arrest us when we came into the city. Since it was impossible to learn what had caused the trouble, Yvette rode to Andersen, Meyer's compound to bring back Mr. Olufsen and his interpreter. She found the whole courtyard swarming with excited Mongol soldiers. A few moments later Olufsen arrived, and we were allowed to return to his house on parole. Then he visited the Foreign Minister, who telephoned the police that we were not to be molested further.

We could never satisfactorily determine what it was all about for every one had a different story. The most plausible explanation was as follows. Russians had been rather *persona non grata* in Urga since the collapse of the empire, and the Mongols were ready to annoy them whenever it was possible to do so and "get away with it." All foreigners are supposed to be Russians by the average native and, when the black Mongol discovered us using a strange machine, he thought it an excellent opportunity to "show off" be-

fore the lamas.   Therefore, he told them that we were
casting a spell over the great temple by means of the
motion picture camera which I was swinging up and
down and from side to side.   This may not be the true
explanation of the trouble but at least it was the one
which sounded most logical to us.

Our lama had been caught in the city, and it was
with difficulty that we were able to obtain his release.
The police charged that he tried to escape when they
ordered him to stop.   He related how they had slapped
his face and pulled his ears before they allowed him to
leave the jail, and he was a very much frightened young
man when he appeared at Andersen, Meyer's compound.   However, he was delighted to have escaped so
easily, as he had had excellent prospects of spending a
week or two in one of the prison coffins.

The whole performance had the gravest possibilities,
and we were exceedingly fortunate in not having been
seriously injured or killed.   By playing upon their superstitions, the black Mongol had so inflamed the lamas
that they were ready for anything.   I should never have
allowed them to separate me from my wife and, to prevent it, probably would have had to use my pistol.   Had
I begun to shoot, death for both of us would have been
inevitable.

The day that we arrived in Urga from the plains we
found the city flooded.   The great square in front of
the horse market was a chocolate-colored lake; a brown
torrent was rushing down the main street; and every
alley was two feet deep in water, or a mass of liquid

mud. It was impossible to walk without wading to
the knees and even our horses floundered and slipped
about, covering us with mud and water. The river
valley, too, presented quite a different picture than
when we had seen it last. Instead of open sweeps of
grassland dotted with an occasional *yurt,* now there
were hundreds of felt dwellings interspersed with tents
of white or blue. It was like the encampment of a
great army, or a collection of huge beehives.

Most of the inhabitants were Mongols from the city
who had pitched their *yurts* in the valley for the summer. Although the wealthiest natives seem to feel
that for the reception of guests their "position" demands a foreign house, they seldom live in it. Duke
Loobitsan Yangsen had completed his mansion the previous winter. It was built in Russian style and furnished with an assortment of hideous rugs and foreign
furniture which made one shiver. But in the yard behind the house his *yurt* was pitched, and there he lived
in comfort.

Loobitsan was a splendid fellow—one of the best
types of Mongol aristocrats. From the crown of his
finely molded head to the toes of his pointed boots, he
was every inch a duke. I saw him in his house one
day reclining on a *kang* while he received half a dozen
minor officials, and his manner of quiet dignity and con-
scious power recalled accounts of the Mongol princes
as Marco Polo saw them. Loobitsan liked foreigners
and one could always find a cordial reception in his

compound. He spoke excellent Chinese and was un-
usually well educated for a Mongol.

Although he was in charge of the customs station
at Mai-ma-cheng and owned considerable property,
which he rented to the Chinese for vegetable gardens,
his chief wealth was in horses. In Mongolia a man's
worldly goods are always measured in horses, not in
dollars. When he needs cash he sells a pony or two
and buys more if he has any surplus silver. His bank
is the open plain; his herdsmen are the guardians of
his riches.

Loobitsan's wife, the duchess, was a nice-looking
woman who seemed rather bored with life. She re-
joiced in two gorgeous strings of pearls, which on state
occasions hung from the silver-encrusted horns of hair
to the shoulders of her brocade jacket. Ordinarily she
appeared in a loose red gown and hardly looked regal.

Loobitsan had never seen Peking and was anxious
to go. When General Hsu Shu-tseng made his *coup
d'état* in November, 1919, Mr. Larsen and Loobitsan
came to the capital as representatives of the Hutukhtu,
and one day, as my wife was stepping into a millinery
shop on Rue Marco Polo, she met him dressed in all
his Mongol splendor. But he was so closely chap-
eroned by Chinese officials that he could not enjoy himself. I saw Larsen not long afterward, and he told me
that Loobitsan was already pining for the open plains
of his beloved Mongolia.

In mid-July, when we returned to Urga, the vegetable season was at its height. The Chinese, of course,

do all the gardening; and the splendid radishes, beets, onions, carrots, cabbages, and beans, which were brought every day to market, showed the wonderful possibilities for development along these lines. North of the Bogdo-ol there is a superabundance of rain and vegetables grow so rapidly in the rich soil that they are deliciously sweet and tender, besides being of enormous size. While we were on the plains our food had consisted largely of meat and we reveled in the change of diet. We wished often for fruit but that is non-existent in Mongolia except a few, hard, watery pears, which merchants import from China.

Mr. Larsen was in Kalgan for the summer but Mr. Olufsen turned over his house and compound for our work. I am afraid we bothered him unmercifully, yet his good nature was unfailing and he was never too busy to assist us in the innumerable details of packing the specimens we had obtained upon the plains and in preparing for our trip into the forests north of Urga. It is men like him who make possible scientific work in remote corners of the world.

CHAPTER XI

MONGOLS AT HOME

Until we left Urga the second time Mongolia, to us, had meant only the Gobi Desert and the boundless, rolling plains. When we set our faces northward we found it was also a land of mountains and rivers, of somber forests and gorgeous flowers.

A new forest always thrills me mightily. Be it of stately northern pines, or a jungle tangle in the tropics, it is so filled with glamour and mystery that I enter it with a delightful feeling of expectation. There is so much that is concealed from view, it is so pregnant with the possibility of surprises, that I am as excited as a child on Christmas morning.

The forests of Mongolia were by no means disappointing. We entered them just north of Urga where the Siberian life zone touches the plains of the central Asian region and the beginnings of a new fauna are sharply delineated by the limit of the trees. We had learned that the Terelche River would offer a fruitful collecting ground. It was only forty miles from Urga and the first day's trip was a delight. We traveled northward up a branch valley enclosed by forested hills and carpeted with flowers. Never had we seen such flowers! Acre after acre of bluebells, forget-me-nots, daisies, buttercups, and cowslips converted the entire valley into a vast "old-fashioned garden," radiantly beautiful. Our camp that night was at the base of a mountain called the Da Wat which shut us off from the Terelche River.

On the second morning, instead of golden sunshine, we awoke to a cloud-hung sky and floods of rain. It was one of those days when everything goes wrong; when with all your heart you wish to swear but instead you must smile and smile and keep on smiling. No one wished to break camp in the icy deluge but there were three marshes between us and the Terelche River which were bad enough in dry weather. A few hours of rain would make them impassable, perhaps for weeks.

My wife and I look back upon that day and the next as one of our few, real hardships. After eight hours of killing work, wet to the skin and almost frozen, we crossed the first dangerous swamp and reached the summit of the mountain. Then the cart, with our most valuable possessions, plunged off the road on a sharp descent and crashed into the forest below. Chen and I escaped death by a miracle and the other Chinese taxidermist, who was safe and sound, promptly had hysterics. It was discouraging, to say the least. We camped in the gathering darkness on a forty-five-degree slope in mud twelve inches deep. Next day we gathered up our scattered belongings, repaired the cart, and reached the river.

I had a letter from Duke Loobitsan Yangsen to a famous old hunter, Tserin Dorchy by name, who lives in the Terelche region. He had been gone for six days on a shooting trip when we came into the beautiful valley where his *yurts* were pitched, but his wife welcomed us with true Mongolian hospitality and a great dish of cheese. Our own camp we made just within the forest, a mile away.

For a week we hunted and trapped in the vicinity, awaiting Tserin Dorchy's return. Our arrival created a deal of interest among the half dozen families in the neighborhood and, after each had paid a formal call, they apparently agreed that we were worthy of being accepted into their community. We were nomads for the time, just as they are for life. We had pitched our tents in the forest, as they had erected their *yurts* in the meadow beside the river. When the biting winds of winter swept the valley a few months later they would move, with all their sheep and goats, to the shelter of the hills and we would seek new hunting grounds.

Before many days we learned all the valley gossip. Moreover, we furnished some ourselves for one of the Chinese taxidermists became enamored of a Mongol maiden. There were two of them, to be exact, and they both "vamped" him persistently. The toilettes with which they sought to allure him were marvels of brilliance, and one of them actually scrubbed her little face and hands with a cake of my yellow, scented soap.

Our servant's affections finally centered upon the younger girl and I smiled paternally upon the wildwood romance. Every night, with a sheepish grin,

Chen would ask to borrow a pony. The responsibilities of chaperones sat lightly on our shoulders, but sometimes my wife and I would wander out to the edge of the forest and watch him to the bottom of the hill. Usually his love was waiting and they would ride off together in the moonlight—where, we never asked!

But we could not blame the boy—those Mongolian nights were made for lovers. The marvel of them we hold among our dearest memories. Wherever we may be, the fragrance of pine trees or the sodden smell of a marsh carries us back in thought to the beautiful valley and fills our hearts again with the glory of its clear, white nights.

No matter what the day brought forth, we looked forward to the evening hunt as best of all. As we trotted our ponies homeward through the fresh, damp air we could watch the shadows deepen in the somber masses of the forest, and on the hilltops see the ragged silhouettes of sentinel pines against the rose glow of the sky. Ribbons of mist, weaving in and out above the stream, clothed the alders in ghostly silver and rested in billowy masses upon the marshes. Ere the moon had risen, the stars blazed out like tiny lanterns in the sky. Over all the valley there was peace unutterable.

We were soon admitted to a delightful comradeship with the Mongols of our valley. We shared their joys and sorrows and nursed their minor ills. First to seek our aid was the wife of the absent hunter, Tserin Dorchy. She rode up one day with a two-year-old baby on her arm. The little fellow was badly infected with eczema, and for three weeks one of the lamas in the tiny temple near their *yurt* had been mumbling prayers and incantations in his behalf, without avail. Fortunately, I had a supply of zinc ointment and before the month was ended the baby was almost well. Then came the lama with his bill "for services rendered," and Tserin Dorchy contributed one hundred dollars to his priestly pocket. A young Mongol with a dislocated shoulder was my next patient, and when I had made him whole, the lama again claimed the credit and collected fifty dollars as the honorarium for his prayers. And so it continued throughout the summer; I made the cures, and the priest got the fees.

Although the Mongols all admitted the efficacy of my foreign medicines, nevertheless they could not bring themselves to dispense with the lama and his prayers. Superstition was too strong and fear that the priest would send an army of evil spirits flocking to their *yurts* if they offended him brought the money, albeit reluctantly, from their pockets. Although the lama never proposed a partnership arrangement, as I thought he might have done, he spent much time about our camp and often brought us bowls of curded milk and cheese. He was a wandering priest and not a permanent resident of the valley, but he evidently decided not to wander any farther until we, too, should leave, for he was with us until the very end.

A short time after we had made our camp near the Terelche River a messenger arrived from Urga with a huge package of mail. In it was a copy of *Harper's*

Magazine containing an account of a flying visit which I had made to Urga in September, 1918.[1]   There were half a dozen Mongols near our tent, among whom was Madame Tserin Dorchy.   I explained the pictures to the hunter's wife in my best Chinese while Yvette "stood by" with her camera and watched results.   Although the woman had visited Urga several times she had never seen a photograph or a magazine and for ten minutes there was no reaction.   Then she recognized a Mongol headdress similar to her own.   With a gasp of astonishment she pointed it out to the others and burst into a perfect torrent of guttural expletives.   A picture of the great temple at Urga, where she once had gone to worship, brought forth another volume of Mongolian adjectives and her friends literally fought for places in the front row.

News travels quickly in Mongolia and during the next week men and women rode in from *yurts* forty or fifty miles away to see that magazine.   I will venture to say that no American publication ever received more appreciation or had a more picturesque audience than did that copy of *Harper's*.

The absent Tserin Dorchy returned one day when I was riding down the valley with his wife.   We saw two strange figures on horseback emerging from the forest, each with a Russian rifle on his back.   Their saddles were strung about with half-dried skins—four roebuck, a musk deer, a moose, and a pair of elk antlers in the "velvet."

---

[1] *Harper's Magazine*, June, 1919, pp. 1-16.

With a joyful shout Madame Tserin Dorchy rode toward her husband. He was an oldish man, of fifty-five years perhaps, with a face as dried and weather-beaten as the leather beneath his saddle. He may have been glad to see her but his only sign of greeting was a *"sai"* and a nod to include us both. Her pleasure was undisguised, however, and as we rode down the valley she chattered volubly between the business of driving in half a dozen horses and a herd of sheep. The monosyllabic replies of the hunter were delivered in a voice which seemed to come from a long way off or from out of the earth beneath his pony's feet. I was interested to see what greeting there would be upon his arrival at the *yurt*. His two daughters and his infant son were waiting at the door but he had not even a word for them and only a pat upon the head for the baby.

All Mongols are independent but Tserin Dorchy was an extreme in every way. He ruled the half dozen families in the valley like an autocrat. What he commanded was done without a question. I was anxious to get away and announced that we would start the day after his arrival. "No," said he, "we will go two days from now." Argument was of no avail. So far as he was concerned, the matter was closed. When it came to arranging wages he stated his terms, which were exorbitant. I could accept them or not as I pleased; he would not reduce his demands by a single copper.

As a matter of fact, offers of money make little impression upon the ordinary Mongols. They produce well-nigh everything they need for they dress in sheep-skins during the winter and eat little else than mutton. When they want cloth, tea, or ammunition, they simply sell a sheep or a pony or barter with the Chinese merchants.

We found that the personal equation enters very largely into any dealings with a Mongol. If he likes you, remuneration is an incident. If he is not interested, money does not tempt him. His independence is a product of the wild, free life upon the plains. He relies entirely upon himself for he has learned that in the struggle for existence, it is he himself that counts. Of the Chinaman, the opposite is true. His life is one of the community and he depends upon his family and his village. He is gregarious above all else and he hates to live alone. In this dependence upon his fellow men he knows that money counts—and there is very little that a Chinaman will not do for money.

On one of his trips across Mongolia, Mr. Coltman's car became badly mired within a stone's throw of a Mongol *yurt*. Two or three oxen were grazing in front of the house and Coltman asked the native to pull his car out of the mud. The Mongol, who was comfortably smoking his pipe in the sun, was not at all interested in the matter, but finally remarked casually that he would do it for eight dollars. There was no argument. Eight dollars was what he said, and eight dollars it would have to be or he would not move. The entire operation of dragging the car to firm ground consumed just four minutes. But this instance was an exception for usually a Mongol is the very essence of good nature and is ready to assist whenever a traveler is in difficulty.

Tserin Dorchy's independence kept us in a constant state of irritation for it was manifested in a dozen different ways. We would gladly have dispensed with his services but his word was law in the community and, if he had issued a "bull" against us, we could not have obtained another man. For all his age, he was an excellent hunter and we came to be good friends.

The old man's independence once led him into serious trouble. He had often looked at the Bogdo-ol with longing eyes and had made short excursions, without his gun, into its sacred forests. On one of these trips he saw a magnificent elk with antlers such as he had never dreamed were carried by any living animal. He could not forget that deer. Its memory was a thorn that pricked him wherever else he hunted. Finally he determined to have it, even if Mongolian law and the Lama Church had proclaimed it sacred.

Toward the end of July, when he deemed the antlers just ripe for plucking, he slipped into the forest during the night and climbed the mountain. After two days he killed the elk. But the lamas who patrol "God's Mountain" had heard the shot and drove him into a great rock-strewn gorge where they lost his trail. Believing that he was still within hearing distance, they shouted to one another that it was useless to hunt longer and that they had best return. Then they concealed themselves and awaited results. An hour later Tserin Dorchy crawled out from under a bowlder directly into their hands.

He had been well-nigh killed before the lamas brought him down to Urga and was still unconscious when they dumped him unceremoniously into one of the prison coffins. He was sentenced to remain a year; but the old man would not have lived a month if Duke Loobitsan Yangsen, with whom he had often hunted, had not obtained his release. His independent spirit is by no means chastened, however, and I feel sure that he will shoot another deer on the Bogdo-ol before he dies!

Three days after his return home, my wife and I left with him and three other Mongols on our first real hunt. Our equipment consisted only of sleeping bags and such food as could be carried on our horses; it was a time when living "close to nature" was really necessary. Eight miles away we stopped at the entrance to a tiny valley. By arranging a bit of canvas over the low branches of a larch tree we prepared a shelter for ourselves and another for the hunters.

In fifteen minutes camp was ready and a fire blazing. When a huge iron basin of water had begun to warm one of the Mongols threw in a handful of brick tea, which resembled nothing so much as powdered tobacco. After the black fluid had boiled vigorously for ten minutes each one filled his wooden eating bowl, put in a great chunk of rancid butter, and then a quantity of finely-ground meal. This is what the Tibetans

call *tsamba,* and the buttered tea was prepared exactly
as we had seen the Tibetans make it. The *tsamba,*
however, was only to enable them to "carry on" until
we killed some game; for meat is the Mongols' "staff
of life," and they care little for anything except animal food.

The evening hunt yielded no results. Two of the
Mongols had missed a bear, I had seen a roebuck, and
the old man had lost a wounded musk deer on the mountain ridge above the camp. But the game was there
and we knew where to find it on the morrow. In the
gray light of early morning Tserin Dorchy and I rode
up the valley through the dew-soaked grass. Once the
old man stopped to examine the rootings of a *ga-hai*
(wild boar), then he continued steadily along the stream
bed. In the half-gloom of the forest the bushes and
trees seemed flat and colorless but suddenly the sun
burned through an horizon cloud, flooding the woods
with golden light. The whole forest seemed instantly to
awaken. It was as though we had come into a dimly
lighted room and touched an electric switch. The trees
and bushes assumed a dozen subtle shades of green,
and the flowers blazed like jewels in the gorgeous wood-
land carpet.

I should have liked to spend the morning in the forest but we knew the deer were feeding in the open. On
foot we climbed upward through knee-high grass to the
summit of a hill. There seemed nothing living in the
meadow but as we walked along the ridge a pair of
grouse shot into the air followed by half a dozen chicks

which buzzed away like brown bullets to the shelter of the trees. We crossed a flat depression and rested for a moment on a rounded hilltop. Below us a new valley sloped downward, bathed in sunshine. Tserin Dorchy wandered slowly to the right while I studied the edge of a marsh with my glasses.

Suddenly I heard the muffled beat of hoofs. Jerking the glasses from my eyes I saw a huge roebuck, crowned with a splendid pair of antlers, bound into view not thirty feet away. For the fraction of a second he stopped, with his head thrown back, then dashed along the hillside. That instant of hesitation gave me just time to seize my rifle, catch a glimpse of the yellow-red body through the rear sight, and fire as he disappeared. Leaping to my feet, I saw four slender legs waving in the air. The bullet had struck him in the shoulder and he was down for good.

My heart pounded with exultation as I lifted his magnificent head. He was the finest buck I had ever seen and I gloated over his body as a miser handles his gold. And gold, shining in the sunlight, was never more beautiful than his spotless summer coat.

Right where he lay upon the hillside, amid a veritable garden of bluebells, daisies, and yellow roses, was the setting for the group we wished to prepare in the American Museum of Natural History. He would be its central figure for his peer could not be found in all Mongolia.

As I stood there in the brilliant sunlight, mentally planning the group, I thought how fortunate I was to have been born a naturalist. A sportsman shoots a deer and takes its head; later, it hangs above his fireplace or in the trophy room. If he be one of imagination, in years to come it will bring back to him the feel of the morning air, the fragrance of the pine trees, and the wild thrill of exultation as the buck went down. But it is a memory picture only and limited to himself. The mounted head can never bring to others the smallest part of the joy he felt and the scene he saw.

The naturalist shares his pleasure and, after all, it is largely that which counts. When the group is constructed in the Museum under his direction he can see reproduced with fidelity and in minutest detail this hidden corner of the world. He can share with thousands of city dwellers the joy of his hunt and teach them something of the animals he loves and the lands they call their own.

To his scientific training he owes another source of pleasure. Every animal is a step in the solution of some one of nature's problems. Perhaps it is a new discovery, a species unknown to science. Asia is full of such surprises—I have already found many. Be the specimen large or small, if it has fallen to your trap or rifle, there is the thrill of knowing that you have traced one more small line on the white portion of nature's map.

While I was gazing at the fallen buck Tserin Dorchy stood like a statue on the hilltop, scanning the forest and valley with the hope that my shot had disturbed another animal. In a few moments he came down to me. The old man had lost some of his accustomed calm and, with thumb upraised, murmured, *"Sai, sai."* Then he gave, in vivid pantomime, a recital of how he suddenly surprised the buck feeding just below the hill crest and how he had seen me jerk the glasses from my eyes and shoot.

Sitting down beside the deer we went through the ceremony of a smoke. Then Tserin Dorchy eviscerated the animal, being careful to preserve the heart, liver, stomach, and intestines. Like all other Orientals with whom I have hunted, the Mongols boiled and ate the viscera as soon as we reached camp and seemed to consider them an especial delicacy.

Some weeks later we killed two elk and Tserin Dorchy inflated and dried the intestines. These were to be used as containers for butter and mutton fat. After tanning the stomach he manufactured from it a bag to contain milk or other liquids. His wife showed me some really beautiful leather which she had made from roebuck skins. Tanning hides and making felt were the only strictly Mongolian industries which we observed in the region visited by our expedition. The Mongols do a certain amount of logging and charcoal burning and in the autumn they cut hay; but with these exceptions we never saw them do any work which could not be done from horseback.

Our first hunting trip lasted ten days and in the following months there were many others. We became typical nomads, spending a day or two in some secluded valley only to move again to other hunting grounds. For the time we were Mongols in all essentials. The primitive instincts, which lie just below the surface in us all, responded to the subtle lure of nature and without an effort we slipped into the care-free life of these children of the woods and plains.

We slept at night under starlit skies in the clean, fresh forest; the first gray light of dawn found us stealing through the dew-soaked grass on the trail of elk, moose, boar or deer; and when the sun was high, like animals, we spent the hours in sleep until the lengthening shadows sent us out again for the evening hunt. In those days New York seemed to be on another planet and very, very far away. Happiness and a great peace was ours, such as those who dwell in cities can never know.

In the midst of our second hunt the Mongols suddenly announced that they must return to the Terelche Valley. We did not want to go, but Tserin Dorchy was obdurate. With the limited Chinese at our command we could not learn the reason, and at the base camp Lü, "the interpreter," was wholly incoherent. "To-morrow, plenty Mongol come," he said. "Riding pony, all same Peking. Two men catch hold, both fall down." My wife was perfectly sure that he had lost his mind, but by a flash of intuition I got his meaning. It was to be a field meet. "Riding pony, all same Peking" meant races, and "two men catch hold, both fall down" could be nothing else than wrestling. I was very proud of myself, and Lü was immensely relieved.

Athletic contests are an integral part of the life of every Mongol community, as I knew, and the members of our valley family were to hold their annual games.

At Urga, in June, the great meet which the Living God blesses with his presence is an amazing spectacle, reminiscent of the pageants of the ancient emperors. All the *élite* of Mongolia gather on the banks of the Tola River, dressed in their most splendid robes, and the archery, wrestling, and horse racing are famous throughout the East.

This love of sport is one of the most attractive characteristics of the Mongols. It is a common ground on which a foreigner immediately has a point of contact. The Chinese, on the contrary, despise all forms of physical exercise. They consider it "bad form," and they do not understand any sport which calls for violent exertion. They prefer to take a quiet walk, carrying their pet bird in a cage for an airing; to play a game of cards; or, if they must travel, to loll back in a sedan chair, with the curtains drawn and every breath of air excluded.

The Terelche Valley meet was held on a flat strip of ground just below our camp. As my wife and I rode out of the forest, a dozen Mongols swept by, gorgeous in flaming red and streaming peacock plumes. They waved a challenge to us, and we joined them in a wild race to a flag in the center of the field. On the side of the hill sat a row of lamas in dazzling yellow gowns; opposite them were the judges, among whom I recognized Tserin Dorchy, though he was so bedecked, behatted and beribboned that I could hardly realize that it was the same old fellow with whom we had lived in camp. (I presume if he saw me in the clothes of civilization he would be equally surprised.)

In front of the judges, who represented the most respected laity of the community, were bowls of cheese cut into tiny cubes. The spectators consisted of two groups of women, who sat some distance apart in compact masses, the "horns" of their headdresses almost interlocked. Their costumes were marvels of brilliance. They looked like a flock of gorgeous butterflies, which had alighted for a moment on the grass.

The first race consisted of about a dozen ponies, ridden by fourteen-year-old boys and girls. They swept up the valley from the starting point in full run, hair streaming, and uttering wailing yells. The winner was led by two old Mongols to the row of lamas, before whom he prostrated himself twice, and received a handful of cheese. This he scattered broadcast, as he was conducted ceremoniously to the judges, from whom he returned with palms brimming with bits of cheese.

Finally, all the contestants in the races, and half a dozen of the Mongols on horseback, lined up in front of the priests, each one singing a barbaric chant. Then they circled about the lamas, beating their horses until they were in a full run. After the race came wrestling matches. The contestants sparred for holds and when finally clinched, each with a grip on the other's waistband, endeavored to obtain a fall by suddenly heaving. When the last wrestling match was finished, a tall Mongol raised the yellow banner, and followed by every man and boy on horseback, circled about the seated lamas. Faster and faster they rode, yelling like demons, and then strung off across the valley to the nearest *yurt*.

Although the sports in themselves were not remarkable, the scene was picturesque in the extreme. Opposite to the grassy hill the forest-clad mountains rose, tier upon tier, in dark green masses. The brilliant yellow lamas faced by the Mongols in their blazing robes and pointed yellow hats, the women, flashing with "jewels" and silver, the half-wild chant, and the rush of horses, gave a barbaric touch which thrilled and fascinated us. We could picture this same scene seven hundred years ago, for it is an ancient custom which has come down from the days of Kublai Khan. It was as though the veil of centuries had been lifted for a moment to allow us to carry away, in motion pictures, this drama of Mongolian life.

CHAPTER XII

NOMADS OF THE FOREST.

Three days after the field meet we left with Tserin Dorchy and two other Mongols for a wapiti hunt. We rode along the Terelche River for three miles, sometimes splashing through the soggy edges of a marsh, and again halfway up a hillside where the ground was firm and hard; then, turning west on a mountain slope, we came to a low plateau which rolled away in undulating sweeps of bush-land between the edges of the dark pine woods. It was a truly boreal landscape; we were on the edge of the forest, which stretches in a vast, rolling sea of green far beyond the Siberian frontier.

From the summit of the table-land we descended between dark walls of pine trees to a beautiful valley filled with parklike openings. Just at dark Tserin Dorchy turned abruptly into the stream and crossed to a pretty grove of spruces on a little island formed by two branches of the river. It was as secluded as a cavern, and made an ideal place in which to camp. A hundred feet away the tent was invisible and, save for the tiny wreaths of smoke which curled above the tree-tops, there was no sign of our presence there.

After dinner Tserin Dorchy shouldered a pack of skins and went to a "salt lick" in a meadow west of camp to spend the night. He returned in the first gray light of dawn, just as I was making coffee, and reported that he had heard wapiti barking, but that no animals had visited the lick. He directed me to go along the hillsides north of camp, while the Mongol hunters struck westward across the mountains.

I had not been gone an hour, and had just worked across the lower end of a deep ravine, when I heard a wapiti bark above and behind me. It was a hoarse roar, exactly like a roebuck, except that it was deeper toned and louder. I was thrilled as though by an electric current. It seemed very far away, much farther than it really was, and as I crept to the summit of a ridge a splendid bull wapiti broke through the underbrush. He had been feeding in the bottom of the ravine and saw my head instantly as it appeared above the sky line. There was no chance to shoot because of the heavy cover; and even when he paused for a moment on the opposite hillside a screen of tree branches was in my way.

Absolutely disgusted with myself, I followed the animal's trail until it was lost in the heavy forest. The wapiti was gone for good, but on the way back to camp I picked up a roebuck which acted as some balm to my injured feelings.

I had climbed to the crest of the mountains enclosing the valley in which we were camped, and was working slowly down the rim of a deep ravine. In my soft leather moccasins I could walk over the springy moss without a sound, and suddenly saw a yellow-red form

moving about in a luxurious growth of grass and tinted
leaves. My heart missed a beat, for I thought it was a
wapiti.

Instantly I dropped behind a bush and, as the animal
moved into the open, I saw it was an enormous roebuck
bearing a splendid pair of antlers. I watched him for
a moment, then aimed low behind the foreleg and fired.
The deer bounded into the air and rolled to the bottom
of the ravine, kicking feebly; my bullet had burst the
heart. It was one of the few times I have ever seen an
animal instantly killed with a heart shot for usually
they run a few yards, and then suddenly collapse.

The buck was almost as large as the first one I had
killed with Tserin Dorchy but it had a twisted right
antler. Evidently it had been injured during the animal's youth and had continued to grow at right angles
to the head, instead of straight up in the normal way.

When I reached camp I found Yvette busily picking
currants in the bushes beside the stream. Her face and
hands were covered with red stains and she looked like
a very naughty little boy who had run away from school
for a day in the woods. Although blueberries grew on
every hillside, we never found strawberries, such as the
Russians in Urga gather on the Bogdo-ol, and only one
patch of raspberries on a burned-off mountain slope.
But the currants were delicious when smothered in
sugar.

Yvette and I rode out to the spot where I had killed
the roebuck to bring it in on Kublai Khan and before
we returned the Mongol hunters had reached camp;

neither of them had seen game of any kind. During the day we discovered some huge trout in the stream almost at our door. We had no hooks or lines, but the Mongols devised a way to catch the fish which brought us food, although it would have made a sportsman shiver. They built a dam of stones across the stream and one man waded slowly along, beating the water with a branch to drive the trout out of the pools into the ripples; then we dashed into the water and tried to catch them with our hands. At least a dozen got away but we secured three by cornering them among the rocks.

They were huge trout, nearly three feet long. Unfortunately I was not able to preserve any of them and I do not know what species they represented. The Mongols and Chinese often catch the same fish in the Tola River by means of nets and we sometimes bought them in Urga. One, which we put on the scales, weighed nine pounds. Although Ted MacCallie tried to catch them with a fly at Urga he never had any success but they probably would take live bait.

August 20 was our second day in camp. At dawn I was awakened by the patter of rain on the tent and soon it became a steady downpour. There was no use in hunting and I went back to sleep. At seven o'clock Chen, who was fussing about the fire, rushed over to say that he could see two wapiti on the opposite mountain. Yvette and I scrambled out of our sleeping bags just in time to see a doe and a fawn silhouetted against the sky rim as they disappeared over the crest. Half an hour later they returned, and I tried a stalk but I lost them in the fog and rain. Tserin Dorchy believed that the animals had gone into a patch of forest on the other side of the mountain. We tried to drive them out but the only thing that appeared was a four-year-old roebuck which the Mongol killed with a single shot.

We had ridden up the mountain by zigzagging across the slope, but when we started back I was astounded to see Tserin Dorchy keep to his saddle. The wet grass was so slippery that I could not even stand erect and half the time was sliding on my back, while Kublai Khan picked his way carefully down the steep descent. The Mongol never left his horse till we reached camp. Sometimes he even urged the pony to a trot and, moreover, had the roebuck strapped behind his saddle. I would not have ridden down that mountain side for all the deer in Mongolia!

It had begun to rain in earnest by eleven o'clock, and we spent a quiet afternoon. There is a charm about a rainy day when one can read comfortably and let it pour. The steady patter on the tent gives one the delightful sensation of immediately escaping extreme discomfort. There is no pleasure in being warm unless the weather is cold; and one never realizes how agreeable it is to be dry unless the day is wet. This day was very wet indeed. We had a month's accumulation of unopened magazines which a Mongol had brought to our base camp just before we left, so there was no chance of being bored. The fire had been built half under a huge, back-log which kept a cheery glow of coals throughout all the downpour, and Chen made us "*chowdzes*"—delicious little balls of meat mixed with onions and seasoned with Chinese sauce. The Mongols slept and ate and slept some more. We ate and slept and read. Therefore, we were very happy.

The weather during that summer in the forest was a source of constant surprise to us. We had never seen such rapid changes from brilliant sunshine to sheets of rain. For an hour or two the sky might stretch above us like a vast blue curtain flecked with tiny masses of snow-white clouds. Suddenly, a leaden blanket would spread itself over every inch of celestial space, while a rush of rain and wind changed the forest to a black chaos of writhing branches and dripping leaves. In fifteen minutes the storm would sweep across the mountain tops, and the sun would again flood our peaceful valley with the golden light of early autumn.

For autumn had already reached us even though the season was only mid-August. It was like October in New York, and we had nightly frosts which withered the countless flowers and turned the leaves to red and gold. In the morning, when I crossed the meadows to the forest, the grass was white with frost and crackled beneath my feet like delicate threads of spun glass. My moccasins were powdered with gleaming crystals of frozen dew, but at the first touch of sun every twig and leaf and blade of grass began to drip, as though from a heavy rain. My feet and legs waist-high were soaked in half an hour, and at the end of the morning hunt I was as wet as though I had waded a dozen rivers.

One cannot move on foot in northern Mongolia without the certainty of a thorough wetting. When the sun has dried the dew, there are swamps and streamlets in every valley and even far up the mountain slopes. It is the heavy rainfall, the rich soil, and the brilliant sunshine that make northern Mongolia a paradise of luxurious grass and flowers, even though the real summer lasts only from May till August. Then, the valleys are like an exquisite garden and the woods are ablaze with color. Bluebells, their stalks bending under the weight of blossoms, clothe every hillside in a glorious azure dress bespangled with yellow roses, daisies, and forget-me-nots. But I think I like the wild poppies best of all, for their delicate, fragile beauty is wonderfully appealing. I learned to love them first in Alaska, where their pale, yellow faces look up happily from the storm-swept hills of the Pribilof Islands in the Bering Sea.

Besides its flowers, this northern country is one of exceeding beauty. The dark green forests of spruce, larch and pine, broken now and then by a grove of poplars or silver birches, the secluded valleys and the rounded hills are strangely restful and give one a sense of infinite peace. It is a place to go for tired nerves. Ragged peaks, towering mountains, and yawning chasms, splendid as they are, may be subtly disturbing, engendering a feeling of restlessness and vague depression. There is none of this in the forests of Mongolia. We felt as though we might be happy there all our lives —the mad rush of our other world seemed very far away and not much worth while.

As yet this land has been but lightly touched by the devastating hand of man. A log road cuts the forest here and there and sometimes we saw a train of ox-carts winding through the trees; but the primitive beauty of the mountains remains unmarred, save where a hillside has been swept by fire. In all our wanderings through the forests we saw no evidences of occupation by the Mongols except the wood roads and a few scattered charcoal pits. These were old and moss-grown, and save for ourselves the valleys were deserted.

One morning while I was hunting north of camp, I heard a wapiti roar on the summit of a mountain. I found its tracks in the soft earth of a game trail which wound through forest so dense that I could hardly see a dozen yards. As I stole along the path I heard a sudden sneeze exactly like that of a human being and saw a small, dark animal dash off the trail. I stopped instantly and slowly sank to the ground, kneeling motionless, with my rifle ready. For five minutes I remained there—the silence of the forest broken only by the clucking of a hazel grouse above my head. Then came that sneeze again, sounding even more human than before. I heard a nervous patter of tiny hoofs, and the animal sneezed from the bushes at my right. I kept as motionless as a statue, and the sneezes followed each other in rapid succession, accompanied by impatient stampings and gentle rustlings in the brush. Then I saw a tiny head emerge from behind a leafy screen and a pair of brilliant eyes gazing at me steadily.

Very, very slowly I raised the rifle until the stock nestled against my cheek; then I fired quickly.

Running to the spot where the head had been I found a beautiful brown-gray animal lying behind a bush. It was no larger than a half-grown fawn, but on either side of its mouth two daggerlike tusks projected, slender, sharp and ivory white. It was a musk deer—the first living, wild one I had ever seen. Even before I touched the body I inhaled a heavy, not unpleasant, odor of musk and discovered the gland upon the abdomen. It was three inches long and two inches wide, but all the hair on the rump and belly was strongly impregnated with the odor.

These little deer are eagerly sought by the natives throughout the Orient, as musk is valuable for perfume. In Urga the Mongols could sell a "pod" for five dollars (silver) and in other parts of China it is worth considerably more. When we were in Yün-nan we frequently heard of a musk buyer whom the Paris perfumer, Pinaud, maintained in the remote mountain village of Atunzi, on the Tibetan frontier.

Because of their commercial value the little animals are relentlessly persecuted in every country which they inhabit and in some places they have been completely exterminated. Those in Mongolia are particularly difficult to kill, since they live only on the mountain summits in the thickest forests. Indeed, were it not for their insatiable curiosity it would be almost impossible ever to shoot them.

They might be snared, of course, but I never saw any

traps or devices for catching animals which the Mongols used; they seem to depend entirely upon their guns. This is quite unlike the Chinese, Koreans, Manchus, Malays, and other Orientals with whom I have hunted, for they all have developed ingenious snares, pitfalls and traps.

The musk sac is present only in the male deer and is, of course, for the purpose of attracting the does. Unfortunately, it is not possible to distinguish the sexes except upon close examination, for both are hornless, and as a result the natives sometimes kill females which they would prefer to leave unmolested.

The musk deer use their tusks for fighting and also to dig up the food upon which they live. I frequently found new pine cones which they had torn apart to get at the soft centers. During the winter they develop an exceedingly long, thick coat of hair which, however, is so brittle that it breaks almost like dry pine needles; consequently, the skins have but little commercial value.

Late one rainy afternoon Tserin Dorchy and I rode into a beautiful valley not far from where we were camped. When well in the upper end, we left our horses and proceeded on foot toward the summit of a ridge on which he had killed a bear a month earlier.

Motioning me to walk to the crest of the ridge from the other side, the old man vanished like a ghost among the trees. When I was nearly at the top I reached the edge of a small patch of burned forest. In the half darkness the charred stumps and skeleton trees were as black as ebony. As I was about to move into the open

I saw an object which at first seemed to be a curiously shaped stump. I looked at it casually, then something about it arrested my attention. Suddenly a tail switched nervously and I realized that the "stump" was an enormous wild boar standing head-on, watching me.

I fired instantly, but even as I pressed the trigger the animal moved and I knew that the bullet would never reach its mark. But my brain could not telegraph to my finger quickly enough to stop its action and the boar dashed away unharmed. It was the largest pig I have ever seen. As he stood on the summit of the ridge he looked almost as big as a Mongol pony. It was too dark to follow the animal so I returned to camp, a very dejected man.

I have never been able to forget that boar and I suppose I never shall. Later, I killed others but they can never destroy the memory of that enormous animal as he stood there looking down at me. Had I realized that it was a pig only the fraction of a second sooner it would have been a different story. But that is the fortune of shooting. In no other sport is the line between success and failure so closely drawn; of course, it is that which makes it so fascinating. At the end of a long day's hunt one chance may be given; then all depends on a clear eye, a steady hand and, above all, judgment. In your action in that single golden second rests the success or failure of, perhaps, a season's trip. You may have traveled thousands of miles, spent hundreds of dollars, and had just one shot at the "head of heads."

Some men tell me that they never get excited when

they hunt. Thank God, I do. There would be no fun at all for me if I *didn't* get excited. But, fortunately, it all comes after the crucial moment. When the stock of the rifle settles against my cheek and I look across the sights, I am as cold as steel. I can shoot, and keep on shooting, with every brain cell concentrated on the work in hand but when it is done, for better or worse, I get the reaction which makes it all worth while.

One morning, a week after we had been in camp, Tserin Dorchy and I discovered a cow and a calf wapiti feeding in an open forest. It was a delight to see how the old Mongol stalked the deer, slipping from tree to bush, sometimes on his knees or flat on his face in the soft moss carpet. When we were two hundred yards away we drew up behind a stump. I took the cow, while Tserin Dorchy covered the calf and at the sound of our rifles both animals went down for good. I was glad to have them for specimens because we never got a shot at a bull in Mongolia, although twice I lost one by the merest chance. One of our hunters brought in a three-year-old moose a short time after we got the wapiti and another had a long chase after a wounded bear.

It was the first week in September when we returned to the base camp, our ponies heavily loaded with skins and antlers. The Chinese taxidermists under my direction had made a splendid collection of small mammals, and we had pretty thoroughly exhausted the resources of the forests in the Terelche region. Therefore, Yvette and I decided that it would be well to ride into Urga and make arrangements for our return to Peking.

We did the fifty miles with the greatest ease and spent the night with Mamen in Mai-ma-cheng. Next day Mr. and Mrs. MacCallie arrived, much to our delight. They were to spend the winter in Urga on business and they brought a supply of much needed ammunition, photographic plates, traps and my Mannlicher rifle. This equipment had been shipped from New York ten months earlier but had only just reached Peking and been released from the Customs through the heroic efforts of Mr. Guptil.

We had another two weeks' hunting trip before we said good-by to Mongolia but it netted few results. All the valleys, which had been deserted when we were there before, were filled with Mongols cutting hay for the winter feed of their sheep and goats. Of course, every camp was guarded by a dog or two, and their continual barking had driven the moose, elk, and bear far back into the deepest forests where we had no time to follow.

Mr. and Mrs. MacCallie had taken a house in Urga, just opposite the Russian Consulate, and they entertained us while I packed our collections which were stored in Andersen, Meyer's godown. It was a full week's work, for we had more than a thousand specimens. The forests of Mongolia had yielded up their treasures as we had not dared to hope they would, and we left them with almost as much regret as we had left the plains.

October first the specimens started southward on camel back. Kublai Khan, my pony, went with them, while we left in the Chinese Government motor cars. For two hundred miles we rushed over the same plains which, a few months earlier, we had laboriously crossed with our caravan. Every spot was pregnant with delightful memories. At this well we had camped for a week and hunted antelope; in that ragged mass of rocks we had killed a wolf; out on the Turin plain we had trapped twenty-six marmots in an enormous colony.

Those had been glorious days and our hearts were sad as we raced back to Peking and civilization. But one bright spot remained—we need not yet leave our beloved East! Far to the south, in brigand-infested mountains on the edge of China, there dwelt a herd of bighorn sheep, the *argali* of the Mongols. Among them was a great ram, and we had learned his hiding place. How we got him is another story.

CHAPTER XIII

THE PASSING OF MONGOLIAN MYSTERY

I know of no other country about which there is so much *misinformation* as about Mongolia. Because the Gobi Desert stretches through its center the popular conception appears to be that it is a waste of sand and gravel incapable of producing anything. In the preceding chapters I have attempted to give a picture of the country as we found it and, although our interests were purely zoölogical, I should like to present a few notes regarding its commercial possibilities, for I have never seen a land which is readily accessible and is yet so undeveloped.

Every year the Far East is becoming increasingly important to the Western World, and especially to the people of the United States, for China and its dependencies is the logical place for the investment of American capital. It is the last great undeveloped field, and I am interested in seeing the American business man appreciate the great opportunities which await him in the Orient.

It is true that the Gobi Desert is a part of Mongolia, but only in its western half is it a desolate waste; in the eastern section it gradually changes into a rolling plain covered with "Gobi sage brush" and short bunch grass.

When one looks closely one sees that the underlying soil is very fine gravel and sand.

There is little water in this region except surface ponds, which are usually dry in summer, and caravans depend upon wells. The water in the desert area contains some alkali but, except in a few instances, the impregnation is so slight that it is not especially disagreeable to the taste. Mr. Larsen told me that there is no part of the country between Kalgan and Urga in which water cannot be found within ten or twenty feet of the surface. I am not prepared to say what this arid region could be made to produce. Doubtless, from the standpoint of agriculture it would be of little importance but sheep and goats could live upon its summer vegetation, I am sure.

It is difficult to say where the Gobi really begins or ends when crossing it between Kalgan and Urga, for the grasslands both on the south and north merge so imperceptibly into the arid central part that there is no real "edge" to the desert; however, it is safe to take Panj-kiang as the southern margin, and Turin as the northern limit, of the Gobi. Both in the north and south the land is rich and fertile—much like the plains of Siberia or the prairies of Kansas and Nebraska.

Such is the eastern Gobi from June to mid-September. In the winter, when the dried vegetation exposes the surface soil, the whole aspect of the country is changed and then it does resemble the popular conception of a desert. But what could be more desertlike than our north China landscape when frost has stripped away the green clothing of its hills and fields?

The Chinese have already demonstrated the agricultural possibilities in the south and every year they reap a splendid harvest of oats, wheat, millet, buckwheat and potatoes. On the grass-covered meadowlands, both north and south of the Gobi, there are vast herds of sheep, goats, cattle and horses, but they are only a fraction of the numbers which the pasturage could support. The cattle and sheep which are exported through China can be sent to Kalgan "on the hoof," for since grass is plentiful, the animals can graze at night and travel during the day. This very materially reduces the cost of transportation.

Besides the great quantities of beef and mutton which could be raised and marketed in the Orient, America or Europe, thousands of pounds of wool and camel hair could be exported. Of course both of these articles are produced at the present time, but only in limited quantities. In the region where we spent the summer, the Mongols sometimes do not shear their sheep or camels but gather the wool from the ground when it has dropped off in the natural process of shedding. Probably half of it is lost, and the remainder is full of dirt and grass which detracts greatly from its value. Moreover, when it is shipped the impurities add at least twenty per cent to its weight, and the high cost of transportation makes this an important factor. Indeed, under proper development the pastoral resources of Mongolia are almost unlimited.

The Turin-Urga region has another commercial asset in the enormous colonies of marmots which inhabit the country for hundreds of miles to the north, east and west. The marmots are prolific breeders—each pair annually producing six or eight young—and, although their fur is not especially fine, it has always been valuable for coats. Several million marmot pelts are shipped every year from Mongolia, the finest coming from Uliassutai in the west, and were American steel traps introduced the number could be doubled.

Urga is just being discovered as a fur market. Many skins which have been taken well across the Russian frontier are sold in Urga, and as the trade increases it will command a still wider area. Wolves, foxes, lynx, bear, wildcats, sables, martens, squirrels and marmots are brought in by thousands; and great quantities of sheep, goat, cow and antelope hides are sent annually to Kalgan. Several foreign fur houses of considerable importance already have their representatives in Urga and more are coming every year. The possibilities for development in this direction are almost boundless, and I believe that within a very few years Urga will become one of the greatest fur markets of the Orient.

As in the south the Chinese farmer cultivates the grasslands of the Mongols, so in the north the Chinese merchant has assumed the trade. Many firms in Peking and Tientsin have branches in Urga and make huge profits in the sale of food, cloth and other essentials to the Mongols and foreigners and in the export of furs, skins and wool. It is well-nigh impossible to touch business in Mongolia at any point without coming in contact with the Chinese.

All work not connected with animals is assumed by Chinese, for the Mongols are almost useless for anything which cannot be done from the back of a horse. Thus the Chinese have a practical monopoly and they exercise all their prerogatives in the enormous prices which they charge for the slightest service. Mongols and foreigners suffer together in this respect, but there is no alternative—the Chinaman can charge what he pleases, for he knows full well that no one else will do the work.

Although there is considerable mineral wealth in northern Mongolia, up to the present time very little prospecting has been done. For several years a Russian company has carried on successful operations for gold at the Yero mines, between Urga and Kiakhta on the Siberian frontier, but they have had to import practically all their labor from China. We often passed Chinese in the Gobi Desert walking across Mongolia pushing a wheelbarrow which contained all their earthly belongings. They were on their way to the Yero mines for the summer's work; in the fall they would return on foot the way they had come. Now that Mongolia is once more a part of the Chinese Republic, the labor problem probably will be improved for there will certainly be an influx of Chinese who are anxious to work.

Transportation is the greatest of all commercial factors in the Orient and upon it largely depends the development of any country. In Mongolia the problem can be easily solved. At the present time it rests upon camel caravans, ox and pony carts and upon automobiles for passengers. Camel traffic begins in September and is virtually ended by the first of June. Then their places on the trail are taken by ox- and pony carts. Camels make the journey from Kalgan to Urga in from thirty to fifty days, but the carts require twice as long. They travel slowly, at best, and the animals must be given time to graze and rest. Of course, they cannot cross the desert when the grass is dry, so that transportation is divided by the season—camels in winter and carts in summer. Each camel carries from four hundred and fifty to five hundred pounds, and the charges for the journey from Kalgan to Urga vary with conditions at from five to fifteen cents (silver) per *cattie* (one and one-third pounds). Thus, by the time goods have reached Urga, their value has increased tremendously.

I can see no reason why motor trucks could not make the trip and am intending to use them on my next expedition. Between Panj-kiang and Turin, the first and third telegraph stations, there is some bad going in spots, but a well made truck with a broad wheel base and a powerful engine certainly could negotiate the sand areas without difficulty. After Turin, where the Gobi may be said to end, the road is like a boulevard.

The motor service for passengers which the Chinese Government maintains between Kalgan and Urga is a sranch of the Peking-Suiyuan Railway and has proved successful after some initial difficulties due to careless and inexperienced chauffeurs. Although the service badly needs organization to make it entirely safe and comfortable, still it has been effective even in its crude form.

At the present time a great part of the business which is done with the Mongols is by barter. The Chinese merchants extend credit to the natives for material which they require and accept in return cattle, horses, hides, wool, etc., to be paid at the proper season. In recent years Russian paper *rubles* and Chinese silver have been the currency of the country, but since the war Russian money has so depreciated that it is now practically valueless. Mongolia greatly needs banking facilities and under the new political conditions undoubtedly these will be materially increased.

A great source of wealth to Mongolia lies in her magnificent forests of pine, spruce, larch and birch which stretch away in an almost unbroken line of green to far beyond the Siberian frontier. As yet but small inroads have been made upon these forests, and as I stood one afternoon upon the summit of a mountain gazing over the miles of timbered hills below me, it seemed as though here at least was an inexhaustible supply of splendid lumber. But no more pernicious term was ever coined than "inexhaustible supply!" I wondered, as I watched the sun drop into the somber masses of the forest, how long these splendid hills would remain inviolate. Certainly not many years after the Gobi Desert has been crossed by lines of steel, and railroad sheds have replaced the gold-roofed temples of sacred Urga.

We are at the very beginning of the days of flying,

and no land which contains such magnificent spruce can keep its treasure boxes unspoiled for very long. Even as I write, aëroplanes are waiting in Peking to make their first flight across Mongolia. The desert nomads have not yet ceased to wonder at the motor cars which cover as many miles of plain in one day as their camels cross in ten. But what *will* they think when twenty men leave Kalgan at noon and dine in Urga at seven o'clock that night! Seven hundred miles mean very little to us now! The start has been made already and, after all, it is largely that which counts. The automobile has come to stay, we know; and motor trucks will soon do for freight what has already been done for passengers, not only from Kalgan to Urga, but west to Uliassutai, and on to Kobdo at the very edge of the Altai Mountains. Few spots in Mongolia need remain untouched, if commercial calls are strong enough.

Last year the first caravans left Feng-chen with wireless equipment for the eighteen hundred mile journey across Mongolia to Urumchi in the very heart of central Asia. Construction at Urga is well advanced and it will soon begin at Kashgar. When these stations are completed Kobdo in Mongolia, Hami in Chinese Turkestan and Sian-fu in Shensi will see wireless shafts erected; and old Peking will be in touch with the remotest spots of her far-flung lands at any time by day or night.

These things are not idle dreams—they are hard business facts already in the first stages of accomplishment. Why, then, should the railroad be long delayed? It may be built from Kalgan to Urga, or by way of Kwei-hua-cheng—either route is feasible. It will mean a direct connection between Shanghai, China's greatest port, and Verkhin Udinsk on the Trans-Siberian Railroad via Tientsin, Peking, Kalgan, Urga, Kiakhta. It will shorten the trip to London by at least four days for passengers and freight. It will open for settlement and commercial development a country of boundless possibilities and unknown wealth which for centuries has been all but forgotten.

Less than seven hundred years ago Mongolia well-nigh ruled the world. Her people were strong beyond belief, but her empire crumbled as quickly as it rose, leaving to posterity only a glorious tradition and a land of mystery. The tradition will endure for centuries; but the motor car and aëroplane and wireless have dispelled the mystery forever.

CHAPTER XIV

THE GREAT RAM OF THE SHANSI MOUNTAINS

Away up in northern China, just south of the Mongolian frontier, is a range of mountains inhabited by bands of wild sheep. They are wonderful animals, these sheep, with horns like battering-rams. But the mountains are also populated by brigands and the two do not form an agreeable combination from the sportsman's standpoint.

In reality they are perfectly nice, well-behaved brigands, but occasionally they forget their manners and swoop down upon the caravan road less than a dozen miles away. This is done only when scouts bring word that cargo valuable enough to make it worth while is about to pass. Each time the brigands make a foray a return raid by Chinese soldiers can be expected. Occasionally these are real, "honest-to-goodness" fights, and blood may flow on both sides, but the battle sometimes takes a different form.

With bugles blowing, the soldiers march out to the hills. Through "middle men" the battle ground has been agreed upon, and a "David" is chosen from the soldiers to meet the "Goliath" of the brigands. But David is particularly careful to leave his gun behind, and to have his "sling" well stuffed with rifle shells.

184

Goliath advances to the combat armed only with a bag of silver dollars. Then an even trade ensues—a dollar for a cartridge—and the implement of war changes hands.

The soldiers return to the city with bugles sounding as merrily as when they left. The commander sends a report to Peking of a desperate battle with the brigands. He says that, through the extreme valor of his soldiers, the bandits have been dispersed and many killed; that hundreds of cartridges were expended in the fight; therefore, kindly send more as soon as possible.

All this because the government has an unfortunate way of forgetting to pay its soldiers in the outlying provinces. When no money is forthcoming and none is visible on the horizon, it is not surprising that they take other means to obtain it. "Battles" of this type are by no means exceptions—they are more nearly the rule in many provinces of China.

But what has all this to do with the wild sheep? Its relation is very intimate, for the presence of brigands in those Shansi mountains has made it possible for the animals to exist. The hunting grounds are only five days' travel from Peking and many foreigners have turned longing eyes toward the mountains. But the brigands always had to be considered. Since Sir Richard Dane, formerly Chief Inspector of the Salt Gabelle, and Mr. Charles Coltman were driven out by the bandits in 1915, the Chinese Government has refused to grant passports to foreigners who wished to shoot in that region. The brigands themselves cannot waste cartridges at one dol-

lar each on the sheep, so the animals have been allowed
to breed unmolested.

Nevertheless, there are not many sheep there. They
are the last survivors of great herds which once roamed
the mountains of north China. The technical name of
the species is *Ovis commosa* (formerly *O. jubata*) and
it is one of the group of bighorns known to sportsmen
by the Mongol name of *argali*. In size, as well as ances-
try, the members of this group are the grandfathers of
all the sheep. The largest ram of our Rocky Mountains is a pygmy compared with a full-grown *argali*.
Hundreds of thousands of years ago the bighorns, which
originated in Asia, crossed into Alaska by way of the
Bering Sea, where there was probably a land connection
at that time. From Alaska they gradually worked
southward, along the mountains of the western coast,
into Mexico and Lower California. In the course of
time, changed environment developed different species;
but the migration route from the Old World to the New
is there for all to read.

The supreme trophy of a sportsman's life is the head
of a Mongolian bighorn sheep. I think it was Rex
Beach who said, "Some men can shoot but not climb.
Some can climb but not shoot. To get a sheep you must
be able to climb and shoot, too."

For its Hall of Asiatic Life, the American Museum
of Natural History needed a group of *argali*. Moreover, we wanted a ram which would fairly represent the
species, and that meant a very big one. The Reverend
Harry R. Caldwell, with whom I had hunted tiger in

south China, volunteered to get them with me. The brigands did not worry us unduly, for we both have had considerable experience with Chinese bandits and we feel that they are like animals—if you don't tease them, they won't bite. In this case the "teasing" takes the form of carrying anything that they could readily dispose of—especially money. I decided that my wife must remain in Peking. She was in open rebellion but there was just a possibility that the brigands might annoy us, and we had determined to have those sheep regardless of consequences.

Although we did not expect trouble, I knew that Harry Caldwell could be relied upon in any emergency. When a man will crawl into a tiger's lair, a tangle of sword grass and thorns, just to find out what the brute has had for dinner; when he will walk into the open in dim light and shoot, with a .22 high-power rifle, a tiger which is just ready to charge; when he will go alone and unarmed into the mountains to meet a band of brigands who have been terrorizing the country, it means that he has more nerve than any one man needs in this life!

After leaving the train at Feng-chen, the journey was like all others in north China; slow progress with a cart over atrocious roads which are either a mass of sticky mud or inches deep in fine brown dust. We had four days of it before we reached the mountains but the trip was full of interest to us both, for along the road there was an ever-changing picture of provincial life. To Harry it was especially illuminating because he had spent nineteen years in south China and had never be-

fore visited the north. He began to realize what every
one soon learns who wanders much about the Middle
Kingdom—that it is never safe to generalize in this
strange land. Conditions true of one region may be
absolutely unknown a few hundred miles away. He
was continually irritated to find that his perfect knowledge of the dialect of Fukien Province was utterly useless. He was well-nigh as helpless as though he had
never been in China, for the languages of the north and
the south are almost as unlike as are French and Ger-
man. Even our "boys" who were from Peking had some
difficulty in making themselves understood, although
we were not more than two hundred miles from the
capital.

Instead of hills thickly clothed with sword grass, here
the slopes were bare and brown. We were too far north
for rice; corn, wheat, and *kaoliang* took the place of
paddy fields. Instead of brick-walled houses we found
dwellings made of clay like the "adobe" of Mexico and
Arizona. Sometimes whole villages were dug into the
hillside and the natives were cave dwellers, spending
their lives within the earth.

All north China is spread with *loess*. During the
Glacial Period, about one hundred thousand years ago,
when in Europe and America great rivers of ice were
descending from the north, central and eastern Asia
seems to have suffered a progressive dehydration. There
was little moisture in the air so that ice could not be
formed. Instead, the climate was cold and dry, while
violent winds carried the dust in whirling clouds for

hundreds upon hundreds of miles, spreading it in ever thickening layers over the hills and plains. Therefore, the "Ice Age" for Europe and America was a "Dust Age" for northeastern Asia.

The inns were a constant source of interest to us both. Their spacious courtyards contrasted strangely with the filthy "hotels" of southern China. In the north all the traffic is by cart, and there must be accommodation for hundreds of vehicles; in the south where goods are carried by boats, coolies, or on donkey back, extensive compounds are unnecessary. Each night, wherever we arrived, we found the courtyard teeming with life and motion. Line after line of laden carts wound in through the wide swinging gates and lined up in orderly array; there was the steady "crunch, crunch, crunch" of feeding animals, shouts for the *jonggweda* (landlord), and good-natured chaffing among the carters. In the great kitchen, which is also the sleeping room, over blazing fires fanned by bellows, pots of soup and macaroni were steaming. On the two great *kangs* (bed platforms), heated from below by long flues radiating outward from the cooking fires, dozens of *mafus* were noisily sucking in their food or already snoring contentedly, rolled in their dusty coats.

Many kinds of folk were there; rich merchants enveloped in splendid sable coats and traveling in padded carts; peddlers with packs of trinkets for the women; wandering doctors selling remedies of herbs, tonics made from deerhorns or tigers' teeth, and wonderful potions of "dragons' bones." Perhaps there was a Buddhist priest or two, a barber, or a tailor. Often a professional entertainer sat cross-legged on the *kang* telling endless stories or singing for hours at a time in a high-pitched, nasal voice, accompanying himself upon a tiny snake-skin violin. It was like a stage drama of concentrated Chinese country life.

Among this polyglot assembly perhaps there may be a single man who has arrived with a pack upon his back. He is indistinguishable from the other travelers and mingles among the *mafus,* helping now and then to feed a horse or adjust a load. But his ears and eyes are open. He is a brigand scout who is there to learn what is passing on the road. He hears all the gossip from neighboring towns as well as of those many miles away, for the inns are the newspapers of rural China, and it is every one's business to tell all he knows. The scout marks a caravan, then slips away into the mountains to report to the leader of his band. The attack may not take place for many days. While the unsuspecting *mafus* are plodding on their way, the bandits are hovering on the outskirts among the hills until the time is ripe to strike.

I have learned that these brigand scouts are my best protection, for when a foreigner arrives at a country inn all other subjects of conversation lose their interest. Everything about him is discussed and rediscussed, and the scouts discover all there is to know. Probably the only things I ever carry which a bandit could use or dispose of readily, are arms and ammunition. But two or three guns are hardly worth the trouble which would follow the death of a foreigner. The brigands know that there would be no sham battle with Chinese soldiers in that event, for the Legations at Peking have a habit of demanding reparation from the Government and insisting that they get it.

As a *raison d'être* for our trip Caldwell and I had been hunting ducks, geese, and pheasants industriously along the way, and not even the "boys" knew our real destination.

We had looked forward with great eagerness to the Tai Hai, a large lake, where it was said that water fowl congregated in thousands during the spring and fall. We reached the lake the second night after leaving Feng-cheng. Darkness had just closed about us when we crossed the summit of a high mountain range and descended into a narrow, winding cut which eventually led us out upon the flat plains of the Tai Hai basin. While we were in the pass a dozen flocks of geese slipped by above our heads, flying very low, the "wedges" showing black against the starlit sky.

With much difficulty we found an inn close beside the lake and, after a late supper, snuggled into our fur bags to be lulled to sleep by that music most dear to a sportsman's heart, the subdued clamor of thousands of waterfowl settling themselves for the night.

At daylight we dressed hurriedly and ran to the lake shore. Harry took a station away from the water at the base of the hills, while I dropped behind three conical mounds which the natives had constructed to obtain salt by evaporation.

I was hardly in position before two geese came straight for me. Waiting until they were almost above my head, I knocked down both with a right and left. The shots put thousands of birds in motion. Flock after flock of geese rose into the air, and long lines of ducks skimmed close to the surface, settling away from shore or on the mud flats near the water's edge.

No more birds came near me, and in fifteen minutes I returned to the inn for breakfast. Harry appeared shortly after with only a mallard duck, for he had guessed wrong as to the direction of the flight, and was entirely out of the shooting.

When the carts had started at eight o'clock Harry and I rode down the shore of the lake to the south, with Chen to hold our horses. The mud flats were dotted with hundreds of ruddy sheldrakes, their beautiful bodies glowing red and gold in the sunlight. A hundred yards from shore half a dozen swans drifted about like floating snow banks, and ducks and geese by thousands rose or settled in the lake. We saw a flock of mallards alight in the short marsh grass and when I fired at least five hundred greenheads, yellow-nibs, and pintails rose in a brown cloud.

Crouched behind the salt mounds, we had splendid shooting and then rode on to join the carts, our ponies loaded with ducks and geese. The road swung about to the north, and we saw geese in tens of thousands coming into the lake across the mountain passes from their summer breeding grounds in Mongolia and far Siberia. Regiment after regiment swept past, circled away to the west, and dropped into the water as though at the command of a field marshal.

Although we were following the main road to Kwei-hua-cheng, a city of considerable importance not far from the mountains which contained the sheep, we had no intention of going there. Neither did we wish to pass through any place where there might be soldiers, so on the last day's march we left the highway and followed an unimportant trail to the tiny village of Wu-shi-tu, which nestles against the mountain's base. Here we made our camp in a Chinese house and obtained two Mongol hunters. We had hoped to live in tents, but there was not a stick of wood for fuel. The natives burn either coal or grass and twigs, but these would not keep us warm in an open camp.

About the village rose a chaotic mass of saw-toothed mountains cut, to the east, by a stupendous gorge. We stood silent with awe, when we first climbed a winding, white trail to the summit of the mountain and gazed into the abysmal depths. My eye followed an eagle which floated across the chasm to its perch on a projecting crag; thence down the sheer face of the cliff a thousand feet to the stream which has carved this colossal cañon from the living rock. Like a shining silver tracing it twisted and turned, foaming over rocks and running in smooth, green sheets between vertical walls of granite. To the north we looked across at a splendid panorama of saw-toothed peaks and ragged pinnacles tinted with delicate shades of pink and lavender. Beneath our feet were slabs of pure white marble and great blocks of greenish feldspar. Among the peaks were deep ravines and, farther to the east, rolling uplands carpeted with grass. There the sheep are found.

We killed only one goral and a roebuck during the first two days, for a violent gale made hunting well-nigh impossible. On the third morning the sun rose in a sky as blue as the waters of a tropic sea, and not a breath of air stirred the silver poplar leaves as we crossed the rocky stream bed to the base of the mountains north of camp. Fifteen hundred feet above us towered a ragged granite ridge which must be crossed ere we could gain entrance to the grassy valleys beyond the barrier.

We had toiled halfway up the slope, when my hunter sank into the grass, pointed upward, and whispered, *"pan-yang"* (wild sheep). There, on the very summit of the highest pinnacle, stood a magnificent ram silhouetted against the sky. It was a stage introduction to the greatest game animal in all the world.

Motionless, as though sculptured from the living granite, it gazed across the valley toward the village whence we had come. Through my glasses I could see every detail of its splendid body—the wash of gray with which many winters had tinged its neck and flanks, the finely drawn legs, and the massive horns curling about a head as proudly held as that of a Roman warrior. He stood like a statue for half an hour, while we crouched motionless in the trail below; then he turned deliberately and disappeared.

When we reached the summit of the ridge the ram was nowhere to be seen, but we found his tracks on a path leading down a knifelike outcrop to the bottom of another valley. I felt sure that he would turn eastward toward the grassy uplands, but Na-mon-gin, my Mongol hunter, pointed north to a sea of ragged mountains. We groaned as we looked at those towering peaks; moreover, it seemed hopeless to hunt for a single animal in that chaos of ravines and cañons.

We had already learned, however, that the Mongol knew almost as much about what a sheep would do as did the animal itself. It was positively uncanny. Perhaps we would see a herd of sheep half a mile away. The old fellow would seat himself, nonchalantly fill his pipe and puff contentedly, now and then glancing at the animals. In a few moments he would announce what was about to happen, and he was seldom wrong.

Therefore, when he descended to the bottom of the valley we accepted his dictum without a protest. At the creek bed Harry and his young hunter left us to follow a deep ravine which led upward a little to the left, while Na-mon-gin and I climbed to the crest by way of a precipitous ridge.

Not fifteen minutes after we parted, Harry's rifle banged three times in quick succession, the reports rolling out from the gorge in majestic waves of sound. A moment later the old Mongol saw three sheep silhouetted for an instant against the sky as they scrambled across the ridge. Then a voice floated faintly up to me from out the cañon.

"I've g o t a f-i-n-e r-a-m," it said, "a b-e-a-u-t-y," and even at that distance I could hear its happy ring.

"Good for Harry," I thought. "He certainly deserved it after his work of last night;" for on the way home his hunter had seen an enormous ram climbing a mountain side and they had followed it to the summit only to lose its trail in the gathering darkness. Harry had stumbled into camp, half dead with fatigue, but with his enthusiasm undiminished.

When Na-mon-gin and I had reached the highest peak and found a trail which led along the mountain side just below the crest, we kept steadily on, now and then stopping to scan the grassy ravines and valleys which radiated from the ridge like the ribs of a giant fan. At half past eleven, as we rounded a rocky shoulder, I saw four sheep feeding in the bottom of a gorge far below us.

Quite unconscious of our presence, they worked out of the ravine across a low spur and into a deep gorge where the grass still showed a tinge of green. As the last one disappeared, we dashed down the slope and came up just above the sheep. With my glasses I could see that the leader carried a fair pair of horns, but that the other three rams were small, as *argali* go.

Lying flat, I pushed my rifle over the crest and aimed at the biggest ram. Three or four tiny grass stems were directly in my line of sight, and fearing that they might deflect my bullet, I drew back and shifted my position a few feet to the right.

One of the sheep must have seen the movement, although we were directly above them, and instantly all were off. In four jumps they had disappeared around a bowlder, giving me time for only a hurried shot at the last one's white rump-patch. The bullet struck a few inches behind the ram, and the valley was empty.

Looking down where they had been so quietly feeding only a few moments before, I called myself all known varieties of a fool. I felt very bad indeed that I had bungled hopelessly my first chance at an *argali*. But the sympathetic old hunter patted me on the shoulder and said in Chinese, "Never mind. They were small ones anyway—not worth having." They were very much worth having to me, however, and all the light seemed to have gone out of the world. We smoked a cigarette, but there was no consolation in that, and I followed the hunter around the peak with a heart as heavy as lead.

Half an hour later we sat down for a look around. I studied every ridge and gully with my glasses without seeing a sign of life. The four sheep had disappeared as completely as though one of the yawning ravines had swallowed them up; the great valley bathed in golden sunlight was deserted and as silent as the tomb.

I was just tearing the wrapper from a piece of chocolate when the hunter touched me on the arm and said quietly, *"Pan-yang li la"* (A sheep has come). He pointed far down a ridge running out at a right angle to the one on which we were sitting, but I could see nothing. Then I scanned every square inch of rock, but still saw no sign of life.

The hunter laughingly whispered, "I can see better

than you can even with your foreign eyes. He is standing in that trail—he may come right up to us."

I tried again, following the thin, white line as it wound from us along the side of the knifelike ridge. Just where it vanished into space I saw the sheep, a splendid ram, standing like a statue of gray-brown granite and gazing squarely at us. He was fully half a mile away, but the hunter had seen him the instant he appeared. Without my glasses the animal was merely a blur to me, but the marvelous eyes of the Mongol could detect its every movement.

"It is the same one we saw this morning," he said. "I was sure we would find him over here. He has very big horns—much better than those others."

That was quite true; but the others had given me a shot and this ram, splendid as he was, seemed as unobtainable as the stars. For an hour we watched him. Sometimes he would turn about to look across the ravines on either side and once he came a dozen feet toward us along the path. The hunter smoked quietly, now and then looking through my glasses. "After a while he will go to sleep," he said, "then we can shoot him."

I must confess that I had but little hope. The ram seemed too splendid and much, much too far away. But I could feast my eyes on his magnificent head and almost count the rings on his curling horns.

A flock of red-legged partridges sailed across from the opposite ridge, uttering their rapid-fire call and alighted almost at our feet. Then each one seemed to melt into the mountain side, vanishing like magic among the grass and stones. I wondered mildly why they had concealed themselves so suddenly, but a moment later there sounded a subdued whir, like the motor of an aëroplane far up in the sky. Three shadows drifted over, and I saw three huge black eagles swinging in ever lowering circles about our heads. I knew then that the partridges had sought the protection of our presence from their mortal enemies, the eagles.

When I looked at the sheep again he was lying down squarely in the trail, lazily raising his head now and then to gaze about. The hunter inspected the ram through my glasses and prepared to go. We rolled slowly over the ridge and then hurried around to the projecting spur at the end of which the ram was lying.

The going was very bad indeed. Pieces of crumbled granite were continually slipping under foot, and at times we had to cling like flies to a wall of rock with a sheer drop of hundreds of feet below us. Twice the Mongol cautiously looked over the ridge, but each time shook his head and worked his way a little farther. At last he motioned me to slide up beside him. Pushing my rifle over the rock before me, I raised myself a few inches and saw the massive head and neck of the ram two hundred yards away. His body was behind a rocky shoulder, but he was looking squarely at us and in a second would be off.

I aimed carefully just under his chin, and at the roar of the high-power shell, the ram leaped backward. "You hit him," said the Mongol, but I felt he must be wrong; if the bullet had found the neck he would have dropped like lead.

Never in all my years of hunting have I had a feeling of such intense surprise and self-disgust. I had been certain of the shot and it was impossible to believe that I had missed. A lump rose in my throat and I sat with my head resting on my hands in the uttermost depths of dejection.

And then the impossible happened! Why it happened, I shall never know. A kind Providence must have directed the actions of the sheep, for, as I raised my eyes, I saw again that enormous head and neck appear from behind a rock a hundred yards away; just that head with its circlet of massive horns and the neck— nothing more. Almost in a daze I lifted my rifle, saw the little ivory bead of the front sight center on that gray neck, and touched the trigger. A thousand echoes crashed back upon us. There was a clatter of stones, a confused vision of a ponderous bulk heaving up and back—and all was still. But it was enough for me; there could be no mistake this time. The ram was mine.

The sudden transition from utter dejection to the greatest triumph of a sportsman's life set me wild with joy. I yelled and pounded the old Mongol on the back until he begged for mercy; then I whirled him about in a war dance on the summit of the ridge. I wanted to leap down the rocks where the sheep had disappeared but the hunter held my arm. For ten minutes we sat there waiting to make sure that the ram would not dash away while we were out of sight in the ravine below. But I knew in my heart that it was all unnecessary. My bullet had gone where I wanted it to go and that was quite enough. No sheep that ever walked could live with a Mannlicher ball squarely in its neck.

When we finally descended, the animal lay halfway down the slope, feebly kicking. What a huge brute he was, and what a glorious head! I had never dreamed that an *argali* could be so splendid. His horns were perfect, and my hands could not meet around them at the base.

Then, of course, I wanted to know what had happened at my first shot. The evidence was there upon his face. My bullet had gone an inch high, struck him in the corner of the mouth, and emerged from his right cheek. It must have been a painful wound, and I shall never cease to wonder what strange impulse brought him back after he had been so badly stung. The second ball had been centered in the neck as though in the bull's-eye of a target.

The skin and head of the sheep made a pack weighing nearly one hundred pounds, and the old Mongol groaned as he looked up at the mountain barriers which separated us from camp. On the summit of the first ridge we found the trail over which we had passed in the morning. Half an hour later the hunter jerked me violently behind a ledge of rock. "*Pan-yang*," he whispered, "there, on the mountain side. Can't you see him?" I could not, and he tried to point to it with my rifle. Just at that instant what I had supposed to be a brown rock came to life in a whirl of dust and vanished into the ravine below.

We waited breathlessly for perhaps a minute—it seemed hours—then the head and shoulders of a sheep appeared from behind a bowlder. I aimed low and fired, and the animal crumpled in its tracks. A second later two rams and a ewe dashed from the same spot and stopped upon the hillside less than a hundred yards away. Instinctively I sighted on the largest but dropped my rifle without touching the trigger. The sheep was small, and even if we did need him for the group we could not carry his head and skin to camp that night. The wolves would surely have found his carcass before dawn, and it would have been a useless waste of life.

The one I had killed was a fine young ram. With the skin, head, and parts of the meat packed upon my shoulders we started homeward at six o'clock. Our only exit lay down the river bed in the bottom of a great cañon, for in the darkness it would have been dangerous to follow the trail along the cliffs. In half an hour it was black night in the gorge. The vertical walls of rock shut out even the starlight, and we could not see more than a dozen feet ahead.

I shall never forget that walk. After wading the stream twenty-eight times I lost count. I was too cold and tired and had fallen over too many rocks to have it make the slightest difference how many more than twenty-eight times we went into the icy water. The hundred-pound pack upon my back weighed more every hour, but the thought of those two splendid rams was as good as bread and wine.

Harry was considerably worried when we reached camp at eleven o'clock, for in the village there had been much talk of bandits. Even before dinner we measured the rams and found that the horns of the one he had killed exceeded the published records for the species by half an inch in circumference. The horns were forty-seven inches in length, but were broken at the tips; the original length was fifty-one inches; the circumference at the base was twenty inches. Moreover, mine was not far behind in size.

As I snuggled into my fur sleeping bag that night, I realized that it had been the most satisfactory hunting day of my life. The success of the group was assured, with a record ram for the central figure. We had three specimens already, and the others would not be hard to get.

The next morning four soldiers were waiting in the courtyard when we awoke. With many apologies they informed us that they had been sent by the commander of the garrison at Kwei-hua-cheng to ask us to go back with them. The mountains were very dangerous; brigands were swarming in the surrounding country; the commandant was greatly worried for our safety. Therefore, would we be so kind as to break camp at once.

We told them politely, but firmly, that it was impossible for us to comply with their request. We needed the sheep for a great museum in New York, and we

could not return without them. As they could see for
themselves our passports had been properly viseed by
the Foreign Office in Peking, and we were prepared to
stay.

The soldiers returned to Kwei-hua-cheng, and the
following day we were honored by a visit from the commandant himself. To him we repeated our determina-
tion to remain. He evidently realized that we could not
be dislodged and suggested a compromise arrangement.
He would send soldiers to guard our house and to accompany us while we were hunting. We assented readily, because we knew Chinese soldiers. Of course, the
sentinel at the door troubled us not at all, and the ones
who were to accompany us were easily disposed of. For
the first day's hunt with our guard we selected the
roughest part of the mountain, and set such a terrific
pace up the almost perpendicular slope that before long
they were left far behind. They never bothered us
again.

CHAPTER XV

MONGOLIAN *ARGALI*

Although we had seen nearly a dozen sheep where we killed our first three rams, the mountains were deserted when Harry returned the following morning. He hunted faithfully, but did not see even a roebuck; the sheep all had left for other feeding grounds. I remained in camp to superintend the preparation of our specimens.

The next day we had a glorious hunt. By six o'clock we were climbing the winding, white trail west of camp, and for half an hour we stood gazing into the gloomy depths of the stupendous gorge, as yet unlighted by the morning sun. Then we separated, each making toward the grassy uplands by different routes.

Na-mon-gin led me along the summit of a broken ridge, but, evidently, he did not expect to find sheep in the ravines, for he kept straight on, mile after mile, with never a halt for rest. At last we reached a point where the plateau rolled away in grassy waves of brown. We were circling a rounded hill, just below the crest, when, not thirty yards away, three splendid roe deer jumped to their feet and stood as though frozen, gazing at us; then, with a snort, they dashed down the slope and up the other side. They had not yet disappeared, when two other bucks crossed a ridge into the bottom of the draw. It was a sore trial to let them go, but the old hunter had his hand upon my arm and shook his head.

Passing the summit of the hill, we sat down for a look around. Before us, nearly a mile away, three shallow, grass-filled valleys dropped steeply from the rolling meadowland. Almost instantly through my binoculars I caught the moving forms of three sheep in the bottom of the central draw. *"Pan-yang,"* I said to the Mongol. "Yes, yes, I see them," he answered. "One has very big horns." He was quite right; for the largest ram carried a splendid head, and the other was by no means small. The third was a tiny ewe. The animals wandered about nibbling at the grass, but did not move out of the valley bottom. After studying them awhile the hunter remarked, "Soon they will go to sleep. We'll wait till then. They would hear or smell us if we went over now."

I ate one of the three pears I had brought for tiffin and smoked a cigarette. The hunter stretched himself out comfortably upon the grass and pulled away at his pipe. It was very pleasant there, for we were protected from the wind, and the sun was delightfully warm. I watched the sheep through the glasses and wondered if I should carry home the splendid ram that night. Finally the little ewe lay down and the others followed her example.

We were just preparing to go when the hunter touched my arm. *"Pan-yang,"* he whispered. "There, coming over the hill. Don't move." Sure enough, a

sheep was trotting slowly down the hillside in our direction. Why he did not see or smell us, I cannot
imagine, for the wind was in his direction. But he
came on, passed within one hundred feet, and stopped
on the summit of the opposite swell. What a shot!
He was so close that I could have counted the rings on
his horns—and they were good horns, too, just the size
we wanted for the group. But the hunter would not
let me shoot. His heart was set upon the big ram
peacefully sleeping a mile away.

"A bird in the hand is worth two in the bush" is a
motto which I have followed with good success in hunting, and I was loath to let that *argali* go even for the
prospect of the big one across the valley. But I had
a profound respect for the opinion of my hunter. He
usually guessed right, and I had found it safe to follow his advice.

So we watched the sheep walk slowly over the crest
of the hill. The Mongol did not tell me then, but he
knew that the animal was on his way to join the others,
and his silence cost us the big ram. You may wonder
how he knew it. I can only answer that what that
Mongol did not know about the ways of sheep was not
worth learning. He seemed to think as the sheep
thought, but, withal, was a most intelligent and delightful companion. His ready sympathy, his keen humor,
and his interest in helping me get the finest specimens
of the animals I wanted, endeared him to me in a way
which only a sportsman can understand. His Shansi
dialect and my limited Mandarin made a curious com-

bination of the Chinese language, but we could always piece it out with signs, and we never misunderstood each other on any important matter.

We had many friendly differences of opinion about the way in which to conduct a stalk, and his childlike glee when he was proved correct was most refreshing. One morning I got the better of him, and for days he could not forget it. We were sitting on a hillside, and with my glasses I picked up a herd of sheep far away on the uplands. "Yes," he said, "one is a very big ram." How he could tell at that distance was a mystery to me, but I did not question his statement for he had proved too often that his range of sight was almost beyond belief.

We started toward the sheep, and after half a mile I looked again. Then I thought I saw a grasscutter, and the animals seemed like donkeys. I said as much but the hunter laughed. "Why, I saw the horns," he said. "One is a big one, a *very* big one." I stopped a second time and made out a native bending over, cutting grass. But I could not convince the Mongol. He disdained my glasses and would not even put them to his eyes. "I don't have to—I *know* they are sheep," he laughed. But I, too, was sure. "Well, we'll see," he said. When we looked again, there could be no mistake; the sheep were donkeys. It was a treat to watch the Mongol's face, and I made much capital of his mistake, for he had so often teased me when I was wrong.

But to return to the sheep across the valley which we were stalking on that sunlit Thursday noon. After the ram had disappeared we made our way slowly around the hilltop, whence he had come, to gain a connecting meadow which would bring us to the ravine where the *argali* were sleeping. On the way I was in a fever of indecision. Ought I to have let that ram go? He was just what we wanted for the group, and something might happen to prevent a shot at the others. It was "a bird in the hand" again, and I had been false to the motto which had so often proved true.

Then the "something" I had feared did happen. We saw a grasscutter with two donkeys emerge from a ravine on the left and strike along the grassy bridge five hundred yards beyond us. If he turned to the right across the upper edge of the meadows, we could whistle for our sheep. Even if he kept straight ahead, possibly they might scent him. The Mongol's face was like a thundercloud. I believe he would have strangled that grasscutter could he have had him in his hands. But the Fates were kind, and the man with his donkeys kept to the left across the uplands. Even then my Mongol would not hurry. His motto was "Slowly, slowly," and we seemed barely to crawl up the slope of the shallow valley which I hoped still held the sheep.

On the summit of the draw the old hunter motioned me behind him and cautiously raised his head. Then a little farther. Another step and a long look. He stood on tiptoe, and, settling back, quietly motioned me to move up beside him.

Just then a gust of wind swept across the hilltop and into the ravine. There was a rush of feet, a clat-

ter of sliding rock, and three *argali* dashed into view
on the opposite slope. They stopped two hundred
yards away. My hunter was frantically whispering,
"One more. Don't shoot. Don't shoot." I was at a
loss to understand, for I knew there were only three
sheep in the draw. The two rams both seemed enormous, and I let drive at the leader. He went down
like lead—shot through the shoulders. The two others
ran a few yards and stopped again. When I fired, the
sheep whirled about but did not fall. I threw in another shell and held the sight well down. The "putt"
of a bullet on flesh came distinctly to us, but the ram
stood without a motion.

The third shot was too much, and he slumped forward, rolled over, and crashed to the bottom of the
ravine. All the time Na-mon-gin was frantically whispering, "Not right. Not right. The big one. The big
one." As the second sheep went down I learned the reason. Out from the valley directly below us rushed a
huge ram, washed with white on the neck and shoulders
and carrying a pair of enormous, curling horns. I was
too surprised to move. How could four sheep be there,
when I knew there were only three!

Usually I am perfectly cool when shooting and have
all my excitement when the work is done, but the un-
expected advent of that ram turned on the thrills a
bit too soon. I forgot what I had whispered to myself
at every shot, "Aim low, aim low. You are shooting
down hill." I held squarely on his gray-white shoulder
and pulled the trigger. The bullet just grazed his

back. He ran a few steps and stopped. Again I fired hurriedly, and the ball missed him by the fraction of an inch. I saw it strike and came to my senses with a jerk; but it was too late, for the rifle was empty. Before I could cram in another shell the sheep was gone.

Na-mon-gin was absolutely disgusted. Even though I had killed two fine rams, he wanted the big one. "But," I said, "where did the fourth sheep come from? I saw only three." He looked at me in amazement. "Didn't you know that the ram which walked by us went over to the others?" he answered. "Any one ought to have known that much."

Well, I hadn't known. Otherwise, I should have held my fire. Right there the Mongol read me a lecture on too much haste. He said I was like every other foreigner—always in a rush. He said a lot of other things which I accepted meekly, for I knew that he was right. I always *am* in a hurry. Missing that ram had taken most of the joy out of the others; and to make matters worse, the magnificent animal stationed himself on the very hillside where we had been sitting when we saw them first and, with the little ewe close beside him, watched us for half an hour.

Na-mon-gin glared at him and shook his fist. "We'll get you to-morrow, you old rabbit," he said; and then to me, "Don't you care. I won't eat till we kill him."

For the next ten minutes the kindly old Mongol devoted himself to bringing a smile to my lips. He told me he knew just where that ram would go; we couldn't have carried in his head anyway; that it would be much better to save him for to-morrow; and that I had killed the other two so beautifully that he was proud of me.

I continued to feel better when I saw the two dead *argali*. They were both fine rams, in perfect condition, with beautiful horns. One of them was the sheep which had walked so close to us; there was no doubt of that, for I had been able to see the details of his "face and figure." Every *argali* has its own special characters which are unmistakable. In the carriage of his head, the curve of his horns, and in coloration, he is as individual as a human being.

While we were examining the sheep, Harry and his hunter appeared upon the rim of the ravine. They brought with them, on a donkey, the skin and head of a fine two-year-old ram which he had killed an hour earlier far beyond us on the uplands. It fitted exactly into our series, and when we had another big ram and two ewes, the group would be complete.

Poor Harry was hobbling along just able to walk. He had strained a tendon in his right leg the previous morning, and had been enduring the most excruciating pain all day. He wanted to stay and help us skin the sheep, but I would not let him. We were a long way from camp, and it would require all his strength to get back at all.

At half-past four we finished with the sheep, and tied the skins and much of the meat on the two donkeys which Harry had commandeered. Our only way home lay down the river bed, for in the darkness we could not follow the trail along the cliffs. By six o'clock it was black night in the gorge.

The donkeys were our only salvation, for by instinct —it couldn't have been sight—they followed the trail along the base of the cliffs. By keeping my hands upon the back of the rearmost animal, and the two Mongols close to me, we got out of the cañon and into the wider valley. When we reached the village I was hungry enough to eat chips, for I had had only three pears since six o'clock in the morning, and it was then nine at night.

Harry, limping into camp just after dark, had met my cousin, Commander Thomas Hutchins, Naval Attaché of the American Legation, and Major Austin Barker of the British Army, whom we had been expecting. They had reached the village about ten o'clock in the morning and spent the afternoon shooting hares near a beautiful temple which Harry had discovered among the hills three miles from camp. The boys had waited dinner for me, and we ate it amid a gale of laughter—we were always laughing during the five days that Tom and Barker were with us.

Harry was out of the hunting the next day because his leg needed a complete rest. I took Tom out with me, while Barker was piloted by an old Mongol who gave promise of being a good hunter. Tom and I climbed the white trail to the summit of the ridge, while Barker turned off to the left to gain the peaks on the other side of the gorge. Na-mon-gin was keen for the big ram which I had missed the day before. He had a very definite impression of just where that sheep was to be found, and he completely ignored the ravines on either side of the trail.

Not half a mile from the summit of the pass, the Mongol stopped and said, *"Pan-yang*—on that ridge across the valley." He looked again and turned to me with a smile. "It is the same ram," he said. "I knew he would be here." Sure enough, when I found the sheep with my glasses, I recognized our old friend. The little ewe was with him, and they had been joined by another ram carrying a circlet of horns, not far short of the big fellow's in size.

For half an hour we watched them while the Mongols smoked. The sheep were standing on the very crest of a ridge across the river, moving a few steps now and then, but never going far from where we first discovered them. My hunter said that soon they would go to sleep, and in less than half an hour they filed down hill into the valley; then we, too, went down, crossed a low ridge, and descended to the river's edge. The climb up the other side was decidedly stiff, and it was nearly an hour before we were peering into the ravine where the sheep had disappeared. They were not there, and the hunter said they had gone either up or down the valley—he could not tell which way.

We went up first, but no sheep. Then we crossed to the ridge where we had first seen the *argali* and cautiously looked over a ledge of rocks. There they were, about three hundred yards below, and on the alert, for they had seen Tom's hunter, who had carelessly exposed himself on the crest of the ridge. Tom fired hurriedly, neglecting to remember that he was shooting down hill, and, consequently, overshot the big ram. They rushed off, two shots of mine falling short at nearly four hundred yards as they disappeared behind a rocky ledge.

My Mongol said that we might intercept them if we hurried, and he led me a merry chase into the bottom of the ravine and up the other side. The sheep were there, but standing in an amphitheater formed by inaccessible cliffs. I advocated going to the ridge above and trying for a shot, but the hunter scoffed at the idea. He said that they would surely scent or hear us long before we could see them.

Tom and his Mongol joined us in a short time, and for an hour we lay in the sunshine waiting for the sheep to compose themselves. It was delightfully warm, and we were perfectly content to remain all the afternoon amid the glorious panorama of encircling peaks.

At last Na-mon-gin prepared to leave. He indicated that we were to go below and that Tom's hunter was to drive the sheep toward us. When we reached the river, the Mongol placed Tom behind a rock at the mouth of the amphitheater. He took me halfway up the slope, and we settled ourselves behind two bowlders.

I was breathing hard from the strenuous climb, and the old fellow waited until I was ready to shoot; then he gave a signal, and Tom's hunter appeared at the very summit of the rocky amphitheater. Instantly the sheep were on the move, running directly toward us. They seemed to be as large as elephants, for never before had I been as close to a living *argali*. Just as the animals mounted the crest of a rocky ledge, not more than fifty yards away, Na-mon-gin whistled sharply, and the sheep stopped as though turned to stone.

"Now," he whispered, "shoot." As I brought my rifle to the level it banged in the air. I had been showing the hunters how to use the delicate set-trigger, and had carelessly left it on. The sheep instantly dashed away, but there was only one avenue of escape, and that was down hill past me. My second shot broke the hind leg of the big ram; the third struck him in the abdomen, low down, and he staggered, but kept on. The sheep had reached the bottom of the valley before my fourth bullet broke his neck.

Tom opened fire when the other ram and the ewe appeared at the mouth of the amphitheater, but his rear sight had been loosened in the climb down the cliff, and his shots went wild. It was hard luck, for I was very anxious to have him kill an *argali*.

The abdomen shot would have finished the big ram eventually, and I might have killed the other before it crossed the creek; but experience has taught me that it is best to take no chances with a wounded animal in rough country such as this. I have lost too many specimens by being loath to finish them off when they were badly hit.

My ram was a beauty. His horns were almost equal to those of the record head which Harry had killed on the first day, but one of them was marred by a broken tip. The old warrior must have weathered nearly a score of winters and have had many battles. But his new coat was thick and fine—the most beautiful of any we had seen. As he lay in the bottom of the valley I was impressed again by the enormous size of an *argali's* body. There was an excellent opportunity to compare it with a donkey's, for before we had finished our smoke, a Mongol arrived driving two animals before him. The sheep was about one-third larger than the donkey, and with his tremendous neck and head must have weighed a great deal more.

After the ram had been skinned Tom and I left the men to pack in the meat, skin, and head, while we climbed to the summit of the pass and wandered slowly home in the twilight. Major Barker came in shortly after we reached the village. He was almost done, for his man had taken him into the rough country north of camp. A strenuous day for a man just from the city, but Barker was enthusiastic. Even though he had not killed a ram, he had wounded one in the leg and had counted twenty sheep—more than either Harry or I had seen during the entire time we had been at Wu-shi-tu.

When we awoke at five o'clock in the morning, Tom stretched himself very gingerly and remarked that the only parts of him which weren't sore were his eyelids! Harry was still *hors de combat* with the strained tendon in his leg, and I had the beginning of an attack of influenza. Barker admitted that his joints "creaked" considerably; still, he was full of enthusiasm. We started off together but separated when six miles from camp. He found sheep on the uplands almost at once, but did not get a head. Barker was greatly handicapped by using a special model U. S. Army Springfield rifle, which weighed almost as much as a machine gun, and could not have been less fitted for hunting in rough country. No man ever worked harder for an *argali* than he did, and he deserved the best head in the mountains. By noon I was burning with fever and almost unable to drag myself back to camp. I arrived at four o'clock, just after Tom returned. He had not seen a sheep.

The Major hunted next day, but was unsuccessful, and none of us went to the mountains again, for I had nearly a week in bed, and Harry was only able to hobble about the court. On the 28th of October, Tom and Barker left for Peking. Harry and I were sorry to have them leave us. I have camped with many men in many countries of the world, but with no two who were better field companions. Neither Harry nor I will ever forget the happy days with them.

It was evident that I could not hunt again for at least a week, although I could sit a horse. We had seven sheep, and the group was assured; therefore, we decided to shift camp to the wapiti country, fifty miles away hoping that by the time we reached there, we both would be fit again.

CHAPTER XVI

THE "HORSE-DEER" OF SHANSI

All the morning our carts had bumped and rattled over the stones in a somber valley one hundred and fifty *li*[1] from where we had killed the sheep. With every mile the precipitous cliffs pressed in more closely upon us until at last the gorge was blocked by a sheer wall of rock. Our destination was a village named Wu-tai-hai, but there appeared to be no possible place for a village in that narrow cañon.

We were a quarter of a mile from the barrier before we could distinguish a group of mud-walled huts, seemingly plastered against the rock like a collection of swallows' nests. No one but a Chinese would have dreamed of building a house in that desolate place. It was Wu-tai-hai, without a doubt, and Harry and I rode forward to investigate.

At the door of a tiny hut we were met by one of our Chinese taxidermists. He ushered us into the court and, with a wave of his hand, announced, "This is the American Legation." The yard was a mass of straw and mud. From the gaping windows of the house bits of torn paper fluttered in the wind; inside, at one end of the largest room, was a bed platform

[1] A *li* equals about one-third of a mile.

219

made of mud; at the other, a fat mother hog with five
squirming "piglets" sprawled contentedly on the dirt
floor. Six years before Colonel (then Captain)
Thomas Holcomb, of the United States Marine Corps,
had spent several days at this hut while hunting elk.
Therefore, it will be known to Peking Chinese until
the end of time as the "American Legation."

An inspection of the remaining houses in the village
disclosed no better quarters, so our boys ousted the
sow and her family, swept the house, spread the *kang*
and floor with clean straw, and pasted fresh paper over
the windows. We longed to use our tents, but there
was nothing except straw or grass to burn, and cooking would be impossible. The villagers were too poor
to buy coal from Kwei-hua-cheng, forty miles away,
and there was not a sign of wood on the bare, brown
hills.

At the edge of the *kang,* in these north Shansi houses,
there is always a clay stove which supports a huge iron
pot. A hand bellows is built into the side of the stove,
and by feeding straw or grass with one hand and ener-
getically manipulating the bellows with the other, a
fire sufficient for simple cooking is obtained.

Except for a few hours of the day the house is as
cold as the yard outside, but the natives mind it not at
all. Men and women alike dress in sheepskin coats
and padded cotton trousers. They do not expect to
remove their clothing when they come indoors, and
warmth, except at night, is a nonessential in their
scheme of life. A system of flues draws the heat from

the cooking fires underneath the *kang*, and the clay bricks retain their temperature for several hours.

At best the north China natives lead a cheerless existence in winter. The house is not a home. Dark, cold, dirty, it is merely a place in which to eat and sleep. There is no home-making instinct in the Chinese wife, for a centuries' old social system, based on the Confucian ethics, has smothered every thought of the privileges of womanhood. Her place is to cook, sew, and bear children; to reflect only the thoughts of her lord and master—to have none of her own.

Wu-tai-hai was typical of villages of its class in all north China; mud huts, each with a tiny courtyard, built end to end in a corner of the hillside. A few acres of ground in the valley bottom and on the mountain side capable of cultivation yield enough wheat, corn, turnips, cabbages, and potatoes to give the natives food. Their life is one of work with few pleasures, and yet they are content because they know nothing else.

Imagine, then, what it meant when we suddenly injected ourselves into their midst. We had come from a world beyond the mountains—a world of which they had sometimes heard, but which was as unreal to them as that of another planet. Europe and America were merely names. A few had learned from passing soldiers that these strange men in that dim, far land had been fighting among themselves and that China, too, was in some vague way connected with the struggle.

But it had not affected them in their tiny rock-bound village. Their world was encompassed within the valley walls or, in its uttermost limits, extended to Kwei-hua-cheng, forty miles away. They knew, even, that a "fire carriage" running on two rails of steel came regularly to Feng-chen, four days' travel to the east, but few of them had ever seen it. So it was almost as unreal as stories of the war and aëroplanes and automobiles.

All the village gathered at the "American Legation" while we unpacked our carts. They gazed in silent awe at our guns and cameras and sleeping bags, but the trays of specimens brought forth an active response. Here was something that was a part of their own life—something they could understand. Mice and rabbits like these they had seen in their own fields; that weasel was the same kind of animal which sometimes stole their chickens. They pointed to the rocks when they saw a red-legged partridge, and told us there were many there; also pheasants.

Why we wanted the skins they could not understand, of course. I told them that we would take them far away across the ocean to America and put them in a great house as large as that hill across the valley; but they smilingly shook their heads. The ocean meant nothing to them, and as for a house as large as a hill—well, there never could be such a place. They were perfectly sure of that.

We had come to Wu-tai-hai to hunt wapiti—*ma-lu* (horse-deer) the natives call them—and they assured us that we could find them on the mountains behind the village. Only last night, said one of the men, he

had seen four standing on the hillside. Two had antlers as long as that stick, but they were no good now
—the horns were hard—we should have come in the
spring when they were soft. Then each pair was worth
$150, at least, and big ones even more. The doctors
make wonderful medicine from the horns—only a little of it would cure any disease no matter how bad it
was. They themselves could not get the *ma-lu,* for the
soldiers had long since taken away all their guns, but
they would show us where they were.

It was pleasant to hear all this, for we wanted some
of those wapiti very badly, indeed. It is one of the
links in the chain of evidence connecting the animals
of the Old World and the New—the problem which
makes Asia the most fascinating hunting ground of all
the earth.

When the early settlers first penetrated the forests
of America they found the great deer which the In-
dians called "wapiti." It was supposed for many years
that it inhabited only America, but not long ago similar
deer were discovered in China, Manchuria, Korea, Mongolia, Siberia, and Turkestan, where undoubtedly the
American species originated. Its white discoverers er-
roneously named the animal "elk," but as this title
properly belongs to the European "moose," sportsmen
have adopted the Indian name "wapiti" to avoid con-
fusion. Of course, changed environment developed
different "species" in all the animals which migrated
from Asia either to Europe or America, but their relationships are very close, indeed.

The particular wapiti which we hoped to get at Wu-tai-hai represented a species almost extinct in China. Because of relentless persecution when the antlers are growing and in the "velvet" and continual cutting of the forests only a few individuals remain in this remote corner of northern Shansi Province. These will soon all be killed, for the railroad is being extended to within a few miles of their last stronghold, and sportsmen will flock to the hills from the treaty ports of China.

Our first hunt was on November first. We left camp by a short cut behind the village and descended to the bowlder-strewn bed of the creek which led into a tremendous gorge. We felt very small and helpless as our eyes traveled up the well-nigh vertical walls to the ragged edge of the chasm a thousand feet above us. The mightiness of it all was vaguely depressing, and it was with a distinct feeling of relief that we saw the cañon widen suddenly into a gigantic amphitheater. In its very center, rising from a ragged granite pedestal, a pinnacle of rock, crowned by a tiny temple, shot into the air. It was three hundred feet, at least, from the stream bed to the summit of the spire—and what a colossal task it must have been to transport the building materials for the temple up the sheer sides of rock! The valley sinners must gain much merit from the danger and effort involved in climbing there to worship.

Farther on we passed two villages and then turned off to the right up a tributary valley. We were anxiously looking for signs of forest, but the only possible cover was in a few ravines where a sparse growth of birch and poplar bushes, not more than six or eight feet high, grew on the north slope. Moreover, we could see that the valley ended in open rolling uplands.

Turning to Na-mon-gin, I said, "How much farther are the *ma-lu?*" "Here," he answered. "We have already arrived. They are in the bushes on the mountain side."

Caldwell and I were astounded. The idea of looking for wapiti in such a place seemed too absurd! There was hardly enough cover successfully to conceal a rabbit, to say nothing of an animal as large as a horse. Nevertheless, the hunters assured us that the *ma-lu* were there, and we began to take a new interest in the birch scrub. Almost immediately we saw three roebuck near the rim of one of the ravines, their white rump-patches showing conspicuously as they bobbed about in the thin cover. We could have killed them easily, but the hunters would not let us shoot, for we were after larger game.

A few moments later we separated, Harry keeping on up the main valley, while my hunter and I turned into a patch of brush directly above us. We had not gone fifty yards when there was a crash, a rush of feet, and four wapiti dashed through the bushes. The three cows kept straight on, but the bull stopped just on the crest of the ridge directly behind a thick screen of twigs. My rifle was sighted at the huge body dimly visible through the branches. In a moment I would have touched the trigger, but the hunter caught my arm, whispering frantically, "Don't shoot! Don't shoot!"

Of course I knew it was a long chance, for the bullet almost certainly would have been deflected by the twigs, but those splendid antlers seemed very near and very, very desirable. I lowered my rifle reluctantly, and the bull disappeared over the hill crest whence the cows had gone.

"They'll stop in the next ravine," said the hunter, but when we cautiously peered over the ridge the animals were not there—nor were they in the next. At last we found their trail leading into the grassy uplands; but the possibility of finding wapiti, these animals of the forests, on those treeless slopes seemed too absurd even to consider. Yet, the old Mongol kept straight on across the rolling meadow.

Suddenly, off at the right, Harry's rifle banged three times in quick succession—then an interval, and two more shots. Ten seconds later three wapiti cows showed black against the sky line. They were coming fast and straight toward us. We flattened ourselves in the grass, lying as motionless as two gray bowlders, and a moment later another wapiti appeared behind the cows. As the sun glistened on his branching antlers there was no doubt that he was a bull, and a big one, too.

The cows were headed to pass about two hundred yards above us and behind the hill crest. I could easily have reached the summit where they would have been at my mercy, but lower down the big bull also was coming, and the hunter would not let me move. "Wait,

wait," he whispered, "we'll surely get him. Wait, we can't lose him."

"What about that ravine?" I answered. "He'll go into the cover. He will never come across this open hillside. I'm going to shoot."

"No, no, he won't turn there. I am sure he won't." The Mongol was right. The big fellow ran straight toward us until he came to the entrance to the valley. My heart was in my mouth as he stopped for an instant and looked down into the cover. Then, for some strange reason, he turned and came on. Three hundred yards away he halted suddenly, swung about, and looked at the ravine again as if half decided to go back.

He was standing broadside, and at the crash of my rifle we could hear the soft thud of the bullet striking flesh; but without a sign of injury he ran forward and stopped under a swell of ground. I could see just ten inches of his back and the magnificent head. It was a small target at three hundred yards, and I missed him twice. With the greatest care I held the little ivory bead well down on that thin brown line, but the bullet only creased his back. It was no use—I simply could not hit him. Running up the hill a few feet, I had his whole body exposed, and the first shot put him down for good.

With a whoop of joy my old Mongol dashed down the steep slope. I had never seen him excited while we were hunting sheep, but now he was wild with delight. Before he had quieted we saw Harry coming over the hill where the wapiti had first appeared. He told us that he had knocked the bull down at long range and had expected to find him dead until he heard me shooting. We found where his bullet had struck the wapiti in the shoulder, yet the animal was running as though untouched.

I examined the bull with the greatest interest, for it was the first Asiatic wapiti of this species that I had ever seen. Its splendid antlers carried eleven points but they were not as massive in the beam or as sharply bent backward at the tips as are those of the American elk. Because of its richer coloration, however, it was decidedly handsomer than any of the American animals.

But the really extraordinary thing was to find the wapiti there at all. It seemed as incongruous as the first automobile that I saw upon the Gobi Desert, for in every other part of the world the animal is a resident of the park-like openings in the forests. Here not a twig or bush was in sight, only the rolling, grass-covered uplands. Undoubtedly these mountains had been wooded many years ago, and as the trees were cut away, the animals had no alternative except to die or adapt themselves to almost plains conditions. The sparse birch scrub in the ravines still afforded them limited protection during the day, but they could feed only at night. It was a case of rapid adaptation to changed environment such as I have seen nowhere else in all the world.

The wapiti, of course, owed their continued exist-

ence to the fact that the Chinese villagers of the valley
had no firearms; otherwise, when the growing antlers
set a price upon their heads, they would all have been
exterminated within a year or two.

CHAPTER XVII

WAPITI, ROEBUCK, AND GORAL

After the first day we left the "American Legation" and moved camp to one of two villages at the upper end of the valley about a mile nearer the hunting grounds. There were only half a dozen huts, but they were somewhat superior to those of Wu-tai-hai, and we were able to make ourselves fairly comfortable. The usual threshing floor of hard clay adjoined each house, and all day we could hear the steady beat, beat, beat, of the flails pounding out the wheat.

The grain was usually freed from chaff by the simple process of throwing it into the air when a brisk wind was blowing, but we saw several hand winnowing machines which were exceedingly ingenious and very effective. The wheat was ground between two circular stones operated by a blindfolded donkey which plodded round and round tied to a shaft. Of course, had the animal been able to see he would not have walked continuously in a circle without giving trouble to his master.

Behind our new house the cliffs rose in sheer walls for hundreds of feet, and red-legged partridges, or chuckars, were always calling from some ledge or bowlder. We could have excellent shooting at almost any hour of the day and often picked up pheasants, bearded partridges, and rabbits in the tiny fields across the stream. Besides the wapiti and roebuck, goral were plentiful on the cliffs and there were a few sheep in the lower valley. Altogether it was a veritable game paradise, but one which I fear will last only a few years longer.

We found that the wapiti were not as easy to kill as the first day's hunt had given us reason to believe. The mountains, separated by deep ravines, were so high and precipitous that if the deer became alarmed and crossed a valley it meant a climb of an hour or more to reach the crest of the new ridge. It was killing work, and we returned to camp every night utterly exhausted.

The concentration of animal life in these scrub-filled gorges was really extraordinary, and I hope that a "game hog" never finds that valley. Probably in no other part of China can one see as many roebuck in a space so limited. It is due, of course, to the unusual conditions. Instead of being scattered over a large area, as is usual in the forest where there is an abundance of cover, the animals are confined to the few ravines in which brush remains. The surrounding open hills isolate them almost as effectively as though they were encircled by water; when driven from one patch of cover they can only run to the next valley.

The facility with which the roebuck and wapiti had adapted themselves to utterly new conditions was a continual marvel to me, and I never lost the feeling of surprise when I saw the animals on the open hillside or running across the rolling, treeless uplands. Had an elephant or a rhinoceros suddenly appeared in place of a deer, it would not have seemed more incongruous.

After we had killed the first wapiti we did not fire a shot for two days, even though roebuck were all about us and we wanted a series for the Museum. This species, *Capreolus bedfordi*, is smaller both in body and in antlers than the one we obtained in Mongolia and differs decidedly in coloration.

On the second hunt I, alone, saw forty-five roebuck, and Harry, who was far to the north of me, counted thirty-one. The third day we were together and put out at least half as many. During that time we saw two wapiti, but did not get a shot at either. Both of us were becoming decidedly tired of passing specimens which we wanted badly and decided to go for roebuck regardless of the possibility of frightening wapiti by the shooting. Na-mon-gin and the other hunters were disgusted with our decision, for they were only interested in the larger game. For the first two drives they worked only half-heartedly, and although seventeen deer were put out of one ravine, they escaped without giving us a shot.

Harry and I held a council of war with the natives and impressed upon them the fact that we were intending to hunt roebuck that day regardless of their personal wishes. They realized that we were not to be dissuaded and prepared to drive the next patch of cover in a really businesslike manner.

Na-mon-gin took me to a position on the edge of a projecting rock to await the natives. As they appeared on the rim of the ravine we saw five roe deer move in the bushes where they had been asleep. Four of them broke back through the line of beaters, but one fine buck came straight toward us. He ran up the slope and crossed a rock-saddle almost beneath me, but I did not fire until he was well away on the opposite hillside; then he plunged forward in his tracks, dead.

Without moving from our position we sent the men over the crest of the mountain to drive the ravines on the other side. The old Mongol and I stretched out upon the rock and smoked for half an hour, while I tried to tell him in my best Chinese—which is very bad —the story of a bear hunt in Alaska. I had just killed the bear, in my narrative, when we saw five roebuck appear on the sky line. They trotted straight toward Harry, and in a moment we heard two shots in quick succession. I knew that meant at least one more deer.

Five minutes later we made out a roebuck rounding the base of the spur on which we sat. It seemed no larger than a brown rabbit at that distance, but the animal was running directly up the bottom of the ravine which we commanded. It was a buck carrying splendid antlers and we watched him come steadily on until he was almost below us.

Na-mon-gin whispered, "Don't shoot until he stops"; but it seemed that the animal would cross the ridge without a pause. He was almost at the summit when he halted for an instant, facing directly away from us. I fired, and the buck leaped backward shot through the neck.

Na-mon-gin was in high good humor, for I had killed two deer with two shots. Harry brought a splendid doe which he had bored neatly through the body as it dashed at full speed across the valley below him. Even the old Mongol had to admit that the wapiti could not have been greatly disturbed by the shooting, and all the men were as pleased as children. There was meat enough for all our boys as well as for the beaters.

Our next day's hunt was for goral on the precipitous cliffs north of camp. Goral belong to a most interesting group of mammals known as the "goat-antelopes" because of the intermediate position which they occupy between the true antelope and the goats. The takin, serow, and goral are the Asiatic members of this sub-family, the *Rupicaprinæ,* which is represented in America by the so-called Rocky Mountain goat and in Europe by the chamois. The goral might be called the Asiatic chamois, for its habits closely resemble those of its European relative.

I had killed twenty-five goral in Yün-nan on the first Asiatic expedition and, therefore, was not particularly keen, from the sporting standpoint, about shooting others. But we did need several specimens, since the north China goral represents a different species, *Nemorhœdus caudatus,* from the one we had obtained in Yün-nan, which is *N. griseus.*

Moreover, Harry was exceedingly anxious to get several of the animals for he had not been very successful with them. He had shot one at Wu-shi-tu, while we were hunting sheep, and after wounding two others at

Wu-tai-hai had begun to learn how hard they are to kill.

The thousand-foot climb up the almost perpendicular cliff was one of the most difficult bits of going which we encountered anywhere in the mountains, and I was ready for a rest in the sun when we reached the summit. Although my beaters were not successful in putting out a goral, we heard Harry shoot once away to the right; and half an hour later I saw him through my binoculars accompanied by one of his men who carried a goral on his shoulders.

On the way Harry disturbed a goral which ran down the sheer wall opposite to us at full speed, bouncing from rock to rock as though made of India rubber. It was almost inconceivable that anything except a bird could move along the face of that cliff, and yet the goral ran apparently as easily as though it had been on level ground. I missed it beautifully and the animal disappeared into a cave among the rocks. Although I sent two bullets into the hole, hoping to drive out the beast, it would not move. Two beaters made their way from above to within thirty feet of the hiding place and sent down a shower of dirt and stones, but still there was no sign of action. Then another native climbed up from below at the risk of his life, and just as he gained the ledge which led to the cave the goral leaped out. The Mongol yelled with fright, for the animal nearly shoved him off the rocks and dashed into the bottom of the ravine where it took refuge in another cave.

I would not have taken that thousand-foot climb

again for all the gorals in China, but Harry started
down at once. The animal again remained in its cave
until a beater was opposite the entrance and then shot
out like an arrow almost into Harry's face. He was
so startled that he missed it twice.

I decided to abandon goral hunting for that day.
Na-mon-gin took me over the summit of the ridge with
two beaters and we found roebuck at once. I returned
to camp with two bucks and a doe. In the lower valley
I met Harry carrying a shotgun and accompanied by
a boy strung about with pheasants and chuckars. After
losing the goral he had toiled up the mountain again
but had found only two roebuck, one of which he shot.

Our second wapiti was killed on November seventh.
It was a raw day with an icy wind blowing across the
ridges where we lay for half an hour while the beaters
bungled a drive for twelve roebuck which had gone into
a scrub-filled ravine. The animals eluded us by running across a hilltop which should have been blocked
by a native, and I got only one shot at a fox. The report of my rifle disturbed eight wapiti which the beaters discovered as they crossed the uplands in the direction of another patch of cover a mile away.

It was a long, cold walk over the hills against the biting wind, and after driving one ravine unsuccessfully
Harry descended to the bottom of a wide valley, while
I continued parallel with him on the summit of the
ridge. Three roebuck suddenly jumped from a shallow ravine in front of me, and one of them, a splendid
buck, stopped behind a bush. It was too great a

temptation, so I fired; but the bullet went to pieces in the twigs and never reached its mark. Harry saw the deer go over the hill and ran around the base of a rocky shoulder just in time to intercept three wapiti which my shot had started down the ravine. He dropped behind a bowlder and let a cow and a calf pass within a few yards of him, for he saw the antlers of a bull rocking along just behind a tiny ridge. As the animal came into view he sent a bullet into his shoulder, and a second ball a few inches behind the first. The elk went down but got to his feet again, and Harry put him under for good with a third shot in the hip.

Looking up he saw another bull, alone, emerging from a patch of cover on the summit of the opposite slope four hundred yards away. He fired point-blank, but the range was a bit too long and his bullet kicked up a cloud of snow under the animal's belly.

I was entirely out of the race on the summit of the hill, for the nearest wapiti was fully eight hundred yards away. Harry's bull was somewhat smaller than the first one we had killed, but had an even more beautiful coat.

We were pretty well exhausted from the week's strenuous climbing and spent Sunday resting and looking after the small mammal work which our Chinese taxidermists had been carrying on under my direction.

Monday morning we were on the hunting grounds shortly after sunrise. At the first drive a beautiful buck roe deer ran out of a ravine into the main valley where I was stationed. Suddenly he caught sight of us where we sat under a rock and stopped with head thrown up and one foot raised. I shall never forget the beautiful picture which he made standing there against the background of snow with the sun glancing on his antlers. Before I could shoot he was off at top speed bounding over the bushes parallel to us. My first shot just creased his back, but the second caught him squarely in the shoulder, while he was in mid-air, turning him over in a complete somersault.

A few moments later we saw the two beaters on the hill run toward each other excitedly and felt sure they had seen something besides roebuck. When they reached us they reported that seven wapiti had run out directly between them and over the ridge.

The climb to the top of the mountain was an ordeal. It was the highest ridge on that side of the valley and every time we reached what appeared to be the crest, another and higher summit loomed above us. We followed the tracks of the animals into a series of ravines which ran down on the opposite side of the mountain and tried a drive. It was too large a territory for our four beaters, and the animals escaped unobserved up one of the valleys. Na-mon-gin and I sat on the hillside for an hour in the icy wind. We were both shaking with cold and I doubt if I could have hit a wapiti if it had stopped fifty feet away.

Harry saw a young elk go into a mass of birch scrub in the bottom of the valley, and when he descended to drive it out, his hunter discovered a huge bull walking slowly up a ravine not two hundred yards from me but under cover of the hill and beyond my sight.

A little before dark we started home by way of a deep ravine which extended out to the main valley. We were talking in a low tone and I was smoking a cigarette —my rifle slung over my shoulder. Suddenly Harry exclaimed, "Great Scott, Roy! There's a *ma-lu*."

On the instant his rifle banged, and I looked up just in time to see a bull wapiti stop on an open slope of the ravine about ninety yards away. Before I had un-slung my rifle Harry fired again, but he could not see the notch in his rear sight and both bullets went high.

Through the peep sight in my Mannlicher the animal was perfectly visible, and when I fired, the bull dropped like lead, rolling over and over down the hill. He attempted to get to his feet but was unable to stand, and I put him down for good with a second shot. It all happened so quickly that we could hardly realize that a day of disappointment had ended in success.

On our way back to camp Harry and I decided that this would end our hunt, for we had three fine bulls, and it was evident that only a very few wapiti remained. The species is doomed to early extinction for, with the advent of the railroad, the last stand which the elk have made by means of their extraordinary adaptation to changed conditions will soon become easily accessible to foreign sportsmen. We at least could keep our consciences clear and not hasten the inevitable day by undue slaughter. In western China other species of wapiti are found in greater numbers, but there can be only one end to the persecution to which they are subjected during the season when they are least able to protect themselves.

It is too much to hope that China will make effective game laws before the most interesting and important forms of her wild life have disappeared, but we can do our best to preserve in museums for future generations records of the splendid animals of the present. Not only are they a part of Chinese history, but they belong to all the world, for they furnish some of the evidence from which it is possible to write the fascinating story of those dim, dark ages when man first came upon the earth.

CHAPTER XVIII

WILD PIGS—ANIMAL AND HUMAN

Shansi Province is famous for wild boar among the sportsmen of China. In the central part there are low mountains and deep ravines thickly forested with a scrub growth of pine and oak. The acorns are a favorite food of the pigs, and the pigs are a favorite food of the Chinese—and of foreigners, too, for that matter. No domestic pork that I have ever tasted can excel a young acorn-fed wild pig! Even a full-grown sow is delicious, but beware of an old boar; not only is he tough beyond description, but his flesh is so "strong" that it annoys me even to see it cooked. I tried to eat some boar meat, once upon a time—that is why I feel so deeply about it.

It is useless to hunt wild pig until the leaves are off the trees, for your only hope is to find them feeding on the hillsides in the morning or early evening. Then they will often come into the open or the thin forests, and you can have a fair shot across a ravine or from the summit of a hill. If they are in the brush it is well-nigh impossible to see them at all. A wild boar is very clever at eluding his pursuers, and for his size can carry off more lead and requires more killing than any other animal of which I know. Therefore, you may be sure of a decidedly interesting hunt. On the other hand, an unsuspecting pig is easy to stalk, for his eyesight is not good; his sense of smell is not much better; and he depends largely upon hearing to protect him from enemies.

In Tientsin and Shanghai there are several sportsmen who year after year go to try for record tusks—they are the real authorities on wild boar hunting. My own experience has been limited to perhaps a dozen pigs killed in Korea, Mongolia, Celebes, and various parts of China.

Harry Caldwell and I returned from our bighorn sheep and wapiti hunt on November 19. He was anxious to go with me for wild boar, but business required his presence in Foochow, and Everett Smith, who had been my companion on a trip to the Eastern Tombs the previous spring, volunteered to accompany me. We left on November 28 by the Peking-Hankow Railroad for Ping-ting-cho, arriving the following afternoon at two o'clock. There we obtained donkeys for pack and riding animals. All the traffic in this part of Shansi is by mules or donkeys. As a result the inns are small, with none of the spacious courtyards which we had found in the north of the province. They were not particularly dirty, but the open coal fires which burned in every kitchen sometimes drove us outside for a breath of untainted air. How it is possible for human beings to exist in rooms so filled with coal gas is beyond my knowledge. Of course, death from gas poisoning is not unusual, but I suppose the natives have become somewhat immune to its effects.

Our destination was a tiny village in the mountains about eight miles beyond Ho-shun, a city of considerable size in the very center of the province. Taiyuan-fu, the capital, at the end of the railway, is a famous place for pigs; but they have been hunted so persistently in recent years that few remain within less than two or three days' journey from the city.

It was a three days' trip from the railroad to Ho-shun, and there was little of interest to distinguish the road from any other in north China. It is always monotonous to travel with pack animals or carts, for they go so slowly that you can make only two or three miles an hour, at best. If there happens to be shooting along the way, as there is in most parts of Shansi, it helps to pass the time. We picked up a few pheasants, some chuckars, and a dozen pigeons, but did not stop to do any real hunting until we entered a wooded valley and established ourselves in a fairly comfortable Chinese hut at the little village of Kao-chia-chuang. On the way in we met a party of Christian Brother missionaries who had been hunting in the vicinity for five days. They had seen ten or twelve pigs and had killed a splendid boar weighing about three hundred and fifty pounds as well as two roebuck.

The mountains near the village had been so thoroughly hunted that there was little chance of finding pigs, but nevertheless we decided to stay for a day or two. I killed a two-year-old roebuck on the first afternoon; and the next morning, while Smith and I were resting on a mountain trail, one of our men saw an enormous wild boar trot across an open ridge and disappear into a heavily forested ravine. I selected a post on a projecting shoulder, while one Chinese went with Smith to pick up the trail of the pig. There were so many avenues of escape open to the boar that I had to remain where it was possible to watch a large expanse of country.

Smith had not yet reached the bottom of the ravine when the native who had remained with me suddenly began to gesticulate wildly and to point to a wooded slope directly in front of us. He hopped about like a man who has suddenly lost his mind and succeeded in keeping in front of me so that I could see nothing but his waving arms and writhing body. Finally seizing him by the collar, I threw him to the ground so violently that he realized his place was behind me. Then I saw the pig running along a narrow trail, silhouetted against the snow which lay thinly on the shaded side of the hill.

He was easily three hundred and fifty yards away and I had little hope of hitting him, but I selected an open patch beyond a bit of cover and fired as he emerged. The boar squealed and plunged forward into the bushes. A moment later he reappeared, zigzagging his way up the slope and only visible through the trees when he crossed a patch of snow. I emptied the magazine of my rifle in a futile bombardment, but the boar crossed the summit and disappeared.

We picked up his bloody trail and for two hours followed it through a tangled mass of scrub and thorns. It seemed certain that we must find him at any moment, for great red blotches stained the snow wherever he stopped to rest. At last the trail led us across an open ridge, and the snow and blood suddenly ceased. We could not follow his footprints in the thick grass and abandoned the chase just before dark.

Two more days of unsuccessful hunting convinced us that the missionaries had driven the pigs to other cover. There was a region twelve miles away to which they might have gone, and we shifted camp to a village named Tziloa a mile or more from the scrub-covered hills which we wished to investigate.

The natives of this part of the country were in no sense hunters. They were farmers who, now that the crops were harvested, had plenty of leisure time and were glad to roam the hills with us. Although their eyesight was remarkable and they were able to see a pig twice as far as we could, they had no conception of stalking the game or of how to hunt it. When we began to shoot, instead of watching the pigs, they were always so anxious to obtain the empty cartridge cases that a wild scramble ensued after every shot. They were like street boys fighting for a penny. It was a serious handicap for successful hunting, and they kept me in such a state of irritation that I never shot so badly in all my life.

We found pigs at Tziloa immediately. The carts went by road to the village, while Smith and I, with two

Chinese, crossed the mountains. On the summit of a ridge not far from the village we met eight native hunters. Two of them had ancient muzzle-loading guns but the others only carried staves. Evidently their method of hunting was to surround the pigs and drive them close up to the men with firearms.

We persuaded one of the Chinese, a boy of eighteen, with cross-eyes and a funny, dried-up little face, to accompany us, for our two guides wished to return that night to Kao-chia-chuang. He led us down a spur which projected northward from the main ridge, and in ten minutes we discovered five pigs on the opposite side of a deep ravine. The sun lay warmly on the slope, and the animals were lazily rooting in the oak scrub. They were a happy family—a boar, a sow, and three half-grown piglets.

We slipped quietly among the trees until we were directly opposite to them and not more than two hundred yards away. The boar and the sow had disappeared behind a rocky corner, and the others were slowly following so that the opportunity for a shot would soon be lost. Telling Smith to take the one on the left, I covered another which stood half facing me. At the roar of my rifle the ravine was filled with wild squeals, and the pig rolled down the hill bringing up against a tree. The boar rushed from behind the rock, and I fired quickly as he stood broadside on. He plunged out of sight, and the gorge was still!

Smith had missed his pig and was very much disgusted. The three Chinese threw themselves down the slope, slipping and rolling over logs and stones, and were up the opposite hill before we reached the bottom of the ravine. They found the pig which I had killed and a blood-splashed trail leading around the hill where the boar had disappeared.

My pig was a splendid male in the rich red-brown coat of adolescence. The bullet had struck him "amidships" and shattered the hip on the opposite side. From the blood on the trail we decided that I had shot the big boar through the center of the body about ten inches behind the forelegs.

We had learned by experience how much killing a full-grown pig required, and had no illusions about finding him dead a few yards away, even though both sides of his path were blotched with red at every step. Therefore, while the Chinese followed the trail, Smith and I sprinted across the next ridge into a thickly forested ravine to head off the boar.

We took stations several yards apart, and suddenly I heard Smith's rifle bang six times in quick succession. The Chinese had disturbed the pig from a patch of cover and it had climbed the opposite hill slope in full view of Smith, who apparently had missed it every time. Missing a boar dodging about among the bushes is not such a difficult thing to do, and although poor Smith was too disgusted even to talk about it, I had a good deal of sympathy for him.

We had little hope of getting the animal when we climbed to the summit of the ridge and saw the tangle of brush into which it had disappeared, but nevertheless we followed the trail which was still showing blood. I was in front and was just letting myself down a snow-covered bowlder, when far below me I saw a huge sow and a young pig walking slowly through the trees. I turned quickly, lost my balance, and slipped feet first over the rock into a mass of thorns and scrub. A locomotive could not have made more noise, and I extricated myself just in time to see the two pigs disappear into a grove of pines. I was bleeding from a dozen scratches, but I climbed to the summit of the ridge and dashed forward hoping to cut them off if they crossed below me. They did not appear, and we tried to drive them out from the cover into which they had made their way; but we never saw them again. It was already beginning to grow dark and too late to pick up the trail of the wounded boar, so we had to call it a day and return to the village.

One of our men carried my shotgun and we killed half a dozen pheasants on the way back to camp. The birds had come into the open to feed, and small flocks were scattered along the valley every few hundred yards. We saw about one hundred and fifty in less than an hour, besides a few chuckars.

I have never visited any part of China where pheasants were so plentiful as in this region. Had we been hunting birds we could have killed a hundred or more without the slightest difficulty during the time we were looking for pigs. We could not shoot, however, without the certainty of disturbing big game and, consequently, we only killed pheasants when on the way back to camp.

During the day the birds kept well up toward the summits of the ridges and only left the cover in the morning and evening.

Our second hunt was very amusing, as well as successful. We met the same party of Chinese hunters early in the morning, and agreed to divide the meat of all the pigs we killed during the day if they would join forces with us. Among them was a tall, fine-looking young fellow, evidently the leader, who was a real hunter—the only one we found in the entire region. He knew instinctively where the pigs were, what they would do, and how to get them.

He led us without a halt along the summit of the mountain into a ravine and up a long slope to the crest of a knifelike ridge. Then he suddenly dropped in the grass and pointed across a cañon to a bare hillside. Two pigs were there in plain sight—one a very large sow. They were fully three hundred yards away and on the edge of a bushy patch toward which they were feeding slowly. Smith left me to hurry to the bottom of the cañon where he could have a shot at close range if either one went down the hill, while I waited behind a stone. Before he was halfway down the slope the sow moved toward the patch of cover into which the smaller pig had already disappeared. It must be then, if I was to have a shot at all. I fired rather hurriedly and registered a clean miss. Both pigs, instead of staying in the cover where they would have been safe, dashed down the open slope toward the bottom of the cañon. At my first shot all eight of the Chinese had leaped for the empty rifle shell and were rolling about like a pack of dogs after a bone. One of them struck my leg just as I fired the second time and the bullet went into the air; I delivered a broadside of my choicest Chinese oaths and the man drew off. I sent three shots after the fleeing sow, but she disappeared unhurt.

One shell remained in my rifle, and I saw the other pig running like a scared rabbit in the very bottom of the cañon. It was so far away that I could barely see the animal through my sights, but when I fired it turned a complete somersault and lay still; the bullet had caught it squarely in the head.

Meanwhile, Smith was having a lively time with the old sow. He had swung around a corner of rock just in time to meet the pig coming at full speed from the other side not six yards away. He tried to check himself, slipped, and sat down suddenly but managed to fire once, breaking the animal's left foreleg. It disappeared into the brush with Smith after it.

He began an intermittent bombardment which lasted half an hour. *Bang, bang, bang*—then silence. *Bang, bang, bang*—silence again. I wondered what it all meant and finally ran down the bottom of the valley until I saw Smith opposite to me just under the rim of the ravine. He was tearing madly through the brush not far behind the sow. As the animal appeared for an instant on the summit of a rise he dropped on one knee and fired twice. Then I saw him race over the hill, leaping the bushes like a roebuck. Once he rolled ten feet into a mass of thorn scrub, but he was up again in an instant, hurdling the brush and fallen logs, his eye on the pig.

It was screamingly funny and I was helpless with laughter. "Go it, Smith," I yelled. "Run him down. Catch him in your hands." He had no breath to waste in a reply, for just then he leaped a fallen log and I saw the sow charge him viciously. The animal had been lying under a tree, almost done, but still had life enough to damage Smith badly if it had reached him. As the man landed on his feet, he fired again at the pig which was almost on him. The bullet caught the brute in the shoulder at the base of the neck and rolled it over, but it struggled to its feet and ran uncertainly a few steps; then it dropped in a little gully.

By the time I had begun to climb the hill Smith shouted that the pig might charge again, and I kept my rifle ready, but the animal was "all in." I circled warily and, creeping up from behind, drove my hunting knife into its heart; even then it struggled to get at me before it rolled over dead.

Smith was streaming blood from a score of scratches, and his clothes were in ribbons, but his face was radiant. "I'd have chased the blasted pig clear to Peking," he said. "All my shells are gone, but I wasn't going to let him get away. If I hadn't kept that last cartridge he'd have caught me, surely."

It was fine enthusiasm and, if ever a man deserved his game, Smith deserved that sow. The animal had been shot in half a dozen places; two legs were broken, and at least three of the bullets had reached vital spots.

Still the brute kept on. Any one who thinks pigs are
easy to kill ought to try the ones in Shansi! The sow
weighed well over three hundred pounds, and it required
six men to carry the two pigs into camp. We got no
more, although we saw two others, but still we felt
that the day had not been ill spent. As long as I live
I shall never forget Smith's hurdle race after that old
sow.

Although I killed two roebuck, the next day I returned to camp with rage in my heart. Smith and I had
separated late in the afternoon, and I was hunting with
an old Chinese when we discovered three pigs—a huge
boar, a sow, and a shote—crossing an open hill. Crawl-
ing on my face, I reached a rock not seventy yards from
the animals. At the first shot the boar pitched over the
bluff into a tangle of thorns, squealing wildly. My
second bullet broke the shoulder of the sow, and I had
a mad chase through a patch of scrub, but finally lost
her.

When I returned to get the big boar I discovered my
Chinese squatted on his haunches in the ravine. He
blandly informed me that the pig could not be found. I
spent the half hour of remaining daylight burrowing in
the thorn scrub without success. I learned later that
the native had concealed the dead pig under a mass of
stones and that during the night he and his *confrères*
had carried it away. Moreover, after we left, they also
got the sow which I had wounded. Although at the time
I did not suspect the man's perfidy, nevertheless it was
apparent that he had not kept his eyes on the boar as I

had told him to do; otherwise the pig could not possibly have escaped.

We had one more day of hunting because Smith had obtained two weeks' leave. The next morning dawned dark and cloudy with spurts of hail—just the sort of weather in which animals prefer to stay comfortably snuggled under a bush in the thickest cover. Consequently we saw nothing all day except one roebuck, which I killed. It was running at full speed when I fired, and it disappeared over the crest of a hill without a sign of injury. Smith was waiting on the other side, and I wondered why he did not shoot, until we reached the summit and discovered the deer lying dead in the grass. Smith had seen the buck plunge over the ridge, and just as he was about to fire, it collapsed.

We found that my bullet had completely smashed the heart, yet the animal had run more than one hundred yards. As it fell, one of its antlers had been knocked off and the other was so loose that it dropped in my hand when I lifted the head. This was on December 11. The other bucks which I had killed still wore their antlers, but probably they would all have been shed before Christmas. The growth takes place during the winter, and the velvet is all off the new antlers by the following May.

On the way back to camp we saw a huge boar standing on an open hillside. Smith and I fired hurriedly and both missed a perfectly easy shot. With one of the Chinese I circled the ridge, while Smith took up the animal's trail. We arrived on the edge of a deep ravine just as the boar appeared in the very bottom. I fired as it rushed through the bushes, and the pig squealed but never hesitated. The second shot struck behind it, but at the third it squealed again and dived into a patch of cover. When we reached the spot we found a great pool of blood and bits of entrails—but no pig. A broad red patch led through the snow, and we followed, expecting at every step to find the animal dead. Instead, the track carried us down the hill, up the bottom of a ravine, and onto a hill bare of snow but thickly covered with oak scrub.

While Smith and I circled ahead to intercept the pig, the Chinese followed the trail. It was almost dark when we went back to the men, who announced that the blood had ceased and that they had lost the track. It seemed incredible; but they had so trampled the trail where it left the snow that we could not find it again in the gloom.

Then Smith and I suspected what we eventually found to be true, viz., that the men had discovered the dead pig and had purposely led us astray. We had no proof, however, and they denied the charge so violently that we began to think our suspicions were unfounded.

We had to leave at daylight next morning in order to reach Peking before Smith's leave expired. Two days after we left, one of my friends arrived at Kao-chia-chuang, where we had first hunted, and reported that the Chinese had brought in all four of the pigs which we had wounded. One of them, probably the boar we lost on the last night, was an enormous animal which the natives said weighed more than five hundred pounds. Of course, this could not have been true, but it probably did reach nearly four hundred pounds.

What Smith and I said when we learned that the scoundrels had cheated us would not look well in print. However, it taught us several things about boar hunting which will prove of value in the future. The Chinese can sell wild pig meat for a very high price since it is considered to be a great delicacy. Therefore, if I wound a pig in the future I shall, myself, follow its trail to the bitter end. Moreover, I learned that, to knock over a wild boar and keep him down for good, one needs a heavy rifle. The bullet of my 6.5 mm. Mannlicher, which has proved to be a wonderful killer for anything up to and including sheep, has not weight enough behind it to stop a pig in its tracks. These animals have such wonderful vitality that, even though shot in a vital spot, they can travel an unbelievable distance. Next time I shall carry a rifle especially designed for pigs and thieving Chinese!

CHAPTER XIX

THE GREAT PARK OF THE EASTERN TOMBS

The sunshine of an early spring day was flooding the flower-filled courtyards of Duke Tsai Tse's palace in Peking when Dr. G. D. Wilder, Everett Smith, and I alighted from our car at the huge brass-bound gate. We came by motor instead of rickshaw, for we were on an official visit which had been arranged by the American Minister. We would have suffered much loss of "face" had we come in any lesser vehicle than an automobile, for we were to be received by a "Royal Highness," an Imperial Duke and a man in whose veins flowed the bluest of Manchu blood. Although living in retirement, Duke Tsai Tse is still a powerful and a respected man.

We were ushered through court after court into a large reception hall furnished in semi-foreign style but in excellent taste. A few moments later the duke entered, dressed in a simple gown of dark blue silk. Had I met him casually on the street I should have known he was a "personality." His high-bred features were those of a maker of history, of a man who has faced the ruin of his own ambitions; who has seen his emperor deposed and his dynasty shattered; but who has lost not one whit of his poise or self-esteem. He carried himself with a quiet dignity, and there was a royal courtesy in his greeting which inspired profound respect. Had he been marked for death in the revolution I am sure that he would have received his executioners in the same calm way that he met us in the reception hall. He listened with a courteous interest while we explained the object of our visit. We had come, we told him, to ask permission to collect natural history specimens in the great hunting park at the *Tung Ling,* Eastern Tombs. Here, and at the *Hsi Ling,* or Western Tombs, the Manchu emperors and their royal consorts sleep in splendid mausoleums among the fragrant pines.

The emperors are buried at the lower end of a vast, walled park, more than one hundred miles in length. True to their reverence for the dead, the Chinese conquerors have never touched these sacred spots, and doubtless will never do so. They belong unquestionably to the Manchus, even if their dynasty has been overthrown by force of arms. According to custom, some member of the royal court is always in residence at the Eastern Tombs. This fact Tsai Tse gravely explained, and said that he would commend us in a letter to Duke Chou, who would be glad to grant us the privileges we asked. Then, by touching his teacup to his lips, he indicated that our interview was ended. With the same courtesy he would have shown to a visiting diplomat he ushered us through the courtyards, while at each doorway we begged him to return. Such is the custom in China. That same afternoon a messenger from the duke arrived at my house in Wu Liang Tajen

Hutung bearing a letter beautifully written in Chinese characters.

Everett Smith and I left next morning for the Eastern Tombs. We went by train to Tung-cho, twelve miles away, where a *mafu* was waiting with our ponies and a cart for baggage. The way to the *Tung Ling* is a delight, for along it north China country life passes before one in panoramic completeness. For centuries this road has been an imperial highway. I could imagine the gorgeous processions that had passed over it and the pomp and ceremony of the visits of the living emperors to the resting places of the dead.

Most vivid of all was the picture in my mind of the last great funeral only nine years ago. I could see the imperial yellow bier slowly, solemnly, borne over the gray Peking hills. In it lay the dead body of the Dowager Empress, Tz'u-hsi—most dreaded yet most beloved —the greatest empress of the last century, the woman who tasted of life and power through the sweetest joys to their bitter core.

We spent the first night at an inn on the outskirts of a tiny village. It was a clean inn, too—very different from those in south China. The great courtyard was crowded with arriving carts. In the kitchen dozens of tired *mafus* were noisily gulping huge bowls of macaroni, and others, stretched upon the *kang,* had already become mere, shapeless bundles of dirty rags. After dinner Smith and I wandered outside the court. An open-air theater was in full operation a few yards from the inn, and all the village had gathered in the street.

But we were of more interest to the audience than the drama itself, and in an instant a score of men and women had surrounded us. They were all good-natured but frankly curious. Finally an old man joined the crowd. "Why," said he, "there are two foreigners!" Immediately the hum of voices ceased, for Age was speaking. "They've got foreign clothes," he exclaimed; "and what funny hats! It is true that foreign hats are much bigger than Chinese caps, and they cost a lot more, too! See that gun the tall one is carrying! He could shoot those pigeons over there as easily as not—all of them with one shot—probably he will in a minute."

The old man continued the lecture until we strolled back to the inn. Undoubtedly he is still discussing us, for there is little to talk about in a Chinese village, except crops and weather and local gossip.

We reached the Eastern Tombs in the late afternoon of the same day. Emerging from a rocky gateway on the summit of a hill, we had the whole panorama of the *Tung Ling* spread out before us. It was like a vast green sea where wave after wave of splendid forests rolled away to the blue haze of distant mountains.

The islands in this forest-ocean were the yellow-roofed tombs, which gave back the sun in a thousand points of golden light. After the monotonous brown of the bare north China hills, the vivid green of the trees was as refreshing as finding an unknown oasis in a sandy desert. To the right was the picturesque village of Malin-yü, the residence of Duke Chou.

From the wide veranda of the charming temple which

we were invited to occupy we could look across the brown village to the splendid park and the glistening yellow roofs of the imperial tombs. We found next day that it is a veritable paradise, a spot of exquisite beauty where profound artistic sentiment has been magnificently expressed. Broad, paved avenues, bordered by colossal animals sculptured in snow-white marble, lead through the trees to imposing gates of red and gold. There is, too, a delightful appreciation of climax. As one walks up a spacious avenue, passing through gate after gate, each more magnificent than the last, one is being prepared by this cumulative splendor for the tomb itself. One feels everywhere the dignity of space. There is no smallness, no crowding. One feels the greatness of the people that has done these things: a race that looks at life and death with a vision as broad as the skies themselves.

At the *Tung Ling* Nature has worked hand in hand with man to produce a harmonious whole. Most of the trees about the tombs have been planted, but the work has been cleverly done. There is nothing glaringly artificial, and you feel as though you were in a well-groomed forest where every tree has grown just where, in Nature's scheme of things, it ought to be.

Although the tombs are alike in general plan, they are, at the same time, as individual as were the emperors themselves. Each is a subtle expression of the character of the one who sleeps beneath the yellow roof. The tomb of Ch'ien-Lung, the artist emperor, lies not far away from that of the Empress Dowager. Stately, beautiful in its simplicity, it is an indication of his life and deeds. In striking contrast is the palace built by the Empress for her eternal dwelling. A woman of iron will, holding her place by force and intrigue, a lover of lavish display—she has expressed it all in her gorgeous tomb. The extravagance of its decoration and the wealth of gold and silver seem to declare to all the world her desire to be known even in death as the greatest of the great. It is said that her tomb cost ten million dollars, and I can well believe it. But a hundred years from now, when Ch'ien-Lung's mausoleum, like the painting of an old master, has grown even more beautiful by the touch of age, that of the Empress will be worn and tarnished.

Charmed with the calm, the peace, the exquisite beauty of the spot, we spent a delightful day wandering among the red and gold pavilions. But fascinating as were the tombs, we were really concerned with the "hinterland," the hunting park itself. Sixty miles to the north, but still within the walls, are towering mountains and glorious forests; these were what we had come to see.

All day, behind three tiny donkeys, we followed a tortuous, foaming stream in the bottom of a splendid valley, ever going upward. At night we slept in the open, and next day crossed the mountain into a forest of oak and pine sprinkled with silver birches. Hundreds of wood-cutters passed us on the trail, each carrying a single log upon his back. Before we reached the village of Shing Lung-shan we came into an area of desolation. Thousands of splendid trees were lying in a chaos of charred and blackened trunks. It was the wantonness of it all that depressed and horrified me.

The reason was perfectly apparent. On every bit of open ground Manchu farmers were at work with plow and hoe. The land was being cleared for cultivation, regardless of all else. North China has very little timber—so little, in fact, that one longs passionately to get away from the bare hills. Yet in this forest-paradise the trees were being sacrificed relentlessly simply to obtain a few more acres on which the farmer could grow his crops. If it had to be done—and Heaven knows it need not have been—the trees might have been utilized for timber. Many have been cut, of course, but thousands upon thousands have been burned simply to clear the hillside.

At Shing Lung-shan we met our hunters and continued up the valley for three hours. With every mile there were fewer open spaces; we had come to a region of vast mountains, gloomy valleys, and heavy forests. The scenery was superb! It thrilled me as did the mountains of Yün-nan and the gorges of the Yangtze. Yet all this grandeur is less than one hundred miles from Peking!

On a little ridge between two foaming streams we made our camp in the forest. From the door of the tent we could look over the tops of the trees into the blue distance of the valley; behind us was a wall of forests broken only by the winding corridor of the mountain torrent.

We had come to the *Tung Ling* especially to obtain specimens of the sika deer (*Cervus hortulorum*) and the Reeves's pheasant (*Syrmaticus reevesi*). The former, a noble animal about the size of our Virginia deer in America, has become exceedingly rare in north China. The latter, one of the most beautiful of living birds, is found now in only two localities—near Ichang on the Yangtze River, and at the *Tung Ling*. When the forests of the Eastern Tombs have been cleared this species will be extinct in all north China.

Early in the morning we left with six hunters. Our way led up the bottom of the valley toward a mountain ridge north of camp. As we walked along the trail, suddenly one of the hunters caught me by the arm and whispered, *"Sang-chi"* (wild chicken). There was a whir of wings, a flash of gold—and I registered a clean miss! The bird alighted on the mountain side, and in the bliss of ignorance Smith and I dashed after it. Ten minutes later we were exhausted from the climb and the pheasant had disappeared. We learned soon that it is useless to chase a Reeves's pheasant when it has once been flushed, for it will invariably make for a mountain side, run rapidly to the top, and, once over the summit, fly to another ridge.

On the way home I got my first pheasant, and an hour later put up half a dozen. I should have had two more, but instead of shooting I only stared, fascinated by the beauty of the thing I saw. It was late in the afternoon and the sun was drawing oblique paths of shimmering golden light among the trees. In a clearing near the summit of a wooded shoulder I saw six pheasants feeding and I realized that, by skirting the base of the ridge, I could slip up from behind and force them to fly across the open valley. The stalk progressed according to schedule. When I crossed the ridge there was a whir of wings and six birds shot into the air not thirty feet away. The sun, glancing on their yellow backs and streaming plumes, transformed them into golden balls, each one with a comet-trail of living fire.

The picture was so indescribably beautiful that I watched them sail across the valley with the gun idle in my hands. Not for worlds would I have turned one of those glorious birds into a crumpled mass of flesh and feathers. For centuries the barred tail plumes, which sometimes are six feet long, have been worn by Chinese actors, and the bird is famous in their literature. It will be a real tragedy when this species has passed out of the fauna of north China, as it will do inevitably if the wanton destruction of the *Tung Ling* forests is continued unchecked.

The next afternoon four sika deer gave me a hard chase up and down three mountain ridges. Finally, we located the animals in a deep valley, and I had an opportunity to examine them through my glasses. Much to my disgust I saw that the velvet was not yet off the antlers and that their winter coats were only partly shed. They were valueless as specimens and forthwith I abandoned the hunt. Before leaving Peking I had visited the zoölogical garden to make sure that the captive sika had assumed their summer dress and antlers. But at the *Tung Ling*, spring had not yet arrived, and the animals were late in losing their winter hair.

In summer the sika is the most beautiful of all deer. Its bright red body, spotted with white, is, when seen among the green leaves of the forest, one of the loveliest things in nature. We wished to obtain a group of these splendid animals for the new Hall of Asiatic Life in the American Museum of Natural History, but the specimens had to be in perfect summer dress.

My hunter was disgusted beyond expression when I refused to shoot the deer. The antlers of the sika when in the velvet are of greater value to the natives than those of any other species. A good pair of horns in full velvet sometimes sells for as much as $450. The growing antlers are called *shueh-chiao* (blood horns) by the Chinese, who consider them of the highest efficacy as a remedy for certain diseases. Therefore, the animals are persecuted relentlessly and very few remain even in the *Tung Ling*.

The antlers of the wapiti are also of great value to the native druggists, but strangely enough they care little for those of the moose and the roebuck. Hundreds of thousand of deerhorns are sent from the interior provinces of China to be sold in the large cities, and the complete extermination of certain species is only a matter of a few decades. Moreover, the female elk, just before the calving season, receive unmerciful persecution, for it is believed that the unborn fawns have great medicinal properties.

Since the roebuck at the *Tung Ling* were in the same
condition as the sika, they were useless for our purposes.
The goral, however, which live high up on the rocky
peaks, had not begun to shed their hair, and they gave
us good shooting. One beautiful morning Smith killed
a splendid ram just above our camp. We had often
looked at a ragged, granite outcrop, sparsely covered
with spruce and pine trees, which towered a thousand
feet above us. We were sure there must be goral somewhere on the ridge, and the hunters told us that they
had sometimes killed them there. It was a stiff climb,
and we were glad to rest when we reached the summit.
The old hunter placed Smith opposite an almost perpendicular face of rock and stationed me beyond him on
the other side. Three beaters had climbed the mountain
a mile below us and were driving up the ridge.

For half an hour I lay stretched out in the sun lux-
uriating in the warmth and breathing in the fragrant
odor of the pines. While I was lazily watching a Chinese green woodpecker searching for grubs in a tree
near by, there came the faintest sound of a loosened
pebble on the cliff above my head. Instantly I was alert
and tense. A second later Smith's rifle banged once.
Then all was still.

In a few moments he shouted to me that he had fired
at a big goral, but that it had disappeared behind the
ridge and he was afraid it had not been hit. The old
hunter, however, had seen the animal scramble into a
tiny grove of pine trees. As it had not emerged, I was
sure the goral was wounded, and when the men climbed

up the cliff they found it dead, bored neatly through the center of the chest.

Gorals, sika, and roebuck are by no means the only big game animals in the *Tung Ling*. Bears and leopards are not uncommon, and occasionally a tiger is killed by the natives. Among other species is a huge flying squirrel, nearly three feet long, badgers, and chipmunks, a beautiful squirrel with tufted ears which is almost black in summer and now is very rare, and dozens of small animals. But perhaps most interesting of all the creatures of these noble forests are the only wild monkeys to be found in northeastern China.

The birds are remarkable in variety and numbers. Besides the Reeves's pheasant, of which I have spoken, there are two other species of this most beautiful family. One, the common ring-necked pheasant, is very abundant; the other is the rare Pucrasia, a gray bird with a dark-red breast, and a yellow striped head surmounted by a conspicuous crest. It is purely a mountain form requiring a mixed forest of pine and oak and, although more widely distributed than the Reeves's pheasant, it occurs in comparatively few localities of north China.

One morning as Smith and I were coming back from hunting we saw our three boys perched upon a ledge above the stream peering into the water. They called to us, "Would you like some fish?" "Of course," we answered, "but how can you get them?"

In a second they had slipped from the rock and were stripping off their clothes. Then one went to the shallows at the lower end of the pool and began to beat the surface with a leafy branch, while the other two crouched on the bowlders in midstream. Suddenly, one of the boys plunged his head and arms into the water and emerged with a beautiful speckled trout clutched tightly in both hands. He had seen the fish swim beneath the rock where it was cornered and had caught it before it could escape.

For an hour the two boys sat like kingfishers, absolutely motionless except when they dived into the water. Of course, they often missed; but when we were ready to go home they had eight beautiful trout, several of them weighing as much as two pounds. The stream was full of fish, and we would have given worlds for a rod and flies.

Lü baked a loaf of corn bread in his curious little oven made from a Standard Oil tin, and we found a jar of honey in our stores. Brook trout fried in deep bacon fat, regular "southern style" corn bread and honey, apple pie, coffee, and cigarettes—the "hardships of camping in the Orient!"

When we had been in camp a week we awoke one morning to find a heavy cloud of smoke drifting up the valley. Evidently a tremendous fire was raging, and Smith and I set out at once on a tour of investigation. A mile down the valley we saw the whole mountain side ablaze. It was a beautiful sight, I admit, but the destruction of that magnificent forest appalled us. Fortunately, the wind was blowing strongly from the east, and there was no danger that the fire might sweep northward in the direction of our camp. As we emerged into a tiny clearing, occupied by a single log hut, we saw two Chinese sitting on their heels, placidly watching the roaring furnace across the valley.

With a good deal of excitement we asked them how the fire possibly could have originated.

"Oh," said one, "we started it ourselves." In the name of the five gods why did you do it?" Smith asked. "Well, you see," returned the Chinese, "there was quite a lot of brush here in our clearing and we had to get rid of it. To-day the wind was right, so we set it on fire."

"But don't you see that you have burned up that whole mountain's side, destroyed thousands of trees, and absolutely ruined this end of the valley?"

"Oh, yes, but never mind; it can't be helped," the native answered. Then I exploded. I frankly confess that I cursed that Chinese and all his ancestors; which is the only proper way to curse in China. I assured him that he was an "old rabbit" and that his father and his grandfather and his great-grandfather were rabbits. To tell a man that he is even remotely connected with a rabbit is decidedly uncomplimentary in China.

But when it was all said I had accomplished nothing. The man looked at me in blank amazement as though I had suddenly lost my mind. He had not the faintest idea that burning up that beautiful forest was reprehensible in the slightest degree. To him and all his kind, the only thing worth while was to clear that bit of land in the valley. If every tree on the mountain was destroyed in the process, what difference did it make? It would be done eventually, anyway. Land, whether it be on a hill or in a valley, was made to grow crops and to be cultivated by Chinese farmers.

The wanton destruction which is being wrought at the *Tung Ling* makes me sick at heart. Here is one of the most beautiful spots in all China, within less than one hundred miles of Peking, which is being ruined utterly as fast as ax and fire can do the work. One can travel the length and breadth of the whole Republic and not find elsewhere so much glorious scenery in so small a space. Moreover, it is the last sanctuary of much of north China's wild life. When the forests of the *Tung Ling* are gone, half a dozen species of birds and mammals will become extinct. How much of the original flora of north China exists to-day only in these forests I would not dare say, for I am not a botanist, but it can be hardly less than the fauna of which I know.

If China could but realize before it is too late how priceless a treasure is being hewed and burned to nothingness and take the first step in conservation by making a National Park of the Eastern Tombs!

Politically there are difficulties, it is true. The *Tung Ling,* and all the surroundings, as I have said, belong unquestionably to the Manchus, and they can do as they wish with their own. But it is largely a question of money, and were the Republic to pay the price for the forests and mountains beyond the Tombs it would not be difficult to do the rest. No country on earth ever had a more splendid opportunity to create for the generations of the present and the future a living memorial to its glorious past.

THE END

INDEX

Aëroplanes, 182

Altai Mountains, 182

American Museum of Natural History, Asiatic Explorations of, vii; trustees of, viii, ix.

Anderson, Dr. J. G., Mining Adviser to Chinese Republic, ix, 39

Anderson, Meyer and Co., assistance rendered to expedition by, ix, 82, 138, 173

Andrews, Yvette B., extract from "Journal" of, 46, 47

Antelope, description of hunt for, 15, 107; speed of, 23, 44, 97, 106, 118

Anthropoides virgo, 11, 42, 55, 88, 91, 93

Argali, 174, 186, 197, 201, 210, 212

Argul, desert fuel, 11, 24, 34

Asia, viii

Asia Magazine, ix

Asian plateau, viii

Asiatic mammals, viii

Asiatic zoölogical explorations, vii

Asses, wild (*Equus hemionus*), 88

Atunzi, 169

Avocets, 42

Baikal Lake, 25

Barker, Major Austin, 213, 215, 217

Beach, Rex, quoted, 186

Bear, 67

Bennett, C. R., ix

Bernheimer, Mr. and Mrs. Charles L., viii

Bighorn sheep (*Argali*), 87, 174, 186

Boar, 67, 171

Bogdo-ol (God's Mountain), 62, 67, 88, 99, 142, 151

Bolsheviki, 25, 32

Bolshevism, xii

Buriats, xiii

Burma, vii, 2

Bustard, 23, 61, 95

Caldwell, Rev. Harry R., 186, 191, 195, 203, 212, 216, 225, 232, 242

Canadian Pacific Ocean Service, transportation to America of collections by, x

Capreolus bedfordi, 232

Caravans, camel, 13, 27, 62, 66, 91

Casarca casarca, 94

Castle, Rev. H., x

Cathay, 1, 64

Cervus hortulorum, 263

271

(2)

www.ingramcontent.com/pod-product-compliance
Lightning Source LLC
Chambersburg PA
CBHW010920040426
42445CB00017B/1923

9 781589 630420